Weaning

ANNABEL KARMEL
Weaning

What to feed, **when** to feed, and **how** to feed your baby

CONTENTS

INTRODUCTION

Welcome to the wonderful world of weaning! Introducing your little one to solids is one of the most magical moments of parenting.

For 26 years, I've been writing books on feeding babies, toddlers, and families, and millions of babies and children worldwide have been brought up on recipes that began their life at my kitchen table. In that time, there has been a lot of research into weaning – in this book, I give you the benefit of that research, as well as nutritious quick and easy recipes and menu planners that will ensure your baby is getting a balanced diet that includes all the nutrients to fuel the rapid growth that takes place in the first year.

In the past, many babies were weaned at four or five months old onto fruit and vegetable purées, and this was fine because a baby's nutritional needs are met by breast or formula milk in the first six months. However, if you introduce solids at around six months, as per the official guidance, fruit and vegetables alone will not give your baby what she needs. In this book, I will guide you through the critical nutrients your baby needs, depending on what age you decide to introduce solids, and how best to provide them.

There are different ways to wean your baby: either the traditional route of giving purées alongside finger foods or by baby-led weaning, a method that gives your baby an element of choice and encourages self-feeding from the outset. I talk you through the pros and cons of each method, but with the reassurance that there is no right or wrong way – every baby is different and you as a parent will be the best judge of what's right for your baby. Many of the recipes in this book can be prepared to suit both methods.

Allergies are a big concern for a lot of parents, which is why I've included an in-depth look at allergies. Many of the recipes can be adapted to take out foods that a child may be allergic to.

I was blessed with three very fussy eaters and for this I am thankful. Had my children been good eaters, I doubt I would ever have written my 44 books or have a global food business, with my ready meals and baby foods, based on some of my most popular recipes, sold in supermarkets. My greatest education has come from what I learned as a mum. My path was not always easy and I lost my first child at three months old – although the reason for this was not diet-related, it became super-important to me to make sure that my children had the best start in life with a healthy diet.

I very much hope that my recipes, tips, and advice will wake up your baby's taste buds, so that she can enjoy and benefit from a positive weaning experience and a healthy diet that will last a lifetime.

Annabel Karmel

Annabel was awarded an MBE by the Queen for her services to child nutrition.

Understanding weaning

The steps involved in **introducing your baby to solid food** are not set in stone and you may find that she progresses more **quickly or more slowly** than other babies of a similar age. **Some days may be better** than others, too, and there will also be times when she wants **only her usual milk.** It helps to understand the basics of weaning and **the theory behind it.** Armed with knowledge, you'll be able to develop a **method that works** for you and your baby.

WHAT WEANING'S ALL ABOUT

Weaning is a gentle process that involves slowly and sensitively replacing your baby's regular milk with nutritious food that will fill her with energy and encourage optimum growth and development. Bear in mind that eating is a learned skill, like walking and talking, and will take time for your baby to master. You have a window of opportunity between 6–12 months of age when your baby will eat pretty well, so take advantage of this to introduce a variety of new flavours that should set her on a path of healthy eating for life.

Your baby's usual milk

From around six months, your baby's regular milk will no longer provide her with all the nutrients she needs – in particular, vitamin D and iron – and her stores of these start becoming depleted by this stage. This is one reason why now is the ideal time to begin weaning, as missing nutrients need to be provided by food. It is, however, very important to remember that your baby's milk will continue to form a significant part of her nutrition for many months to come, giving her the fats, carbohydrates, protein, vitamins, and minerals she needs. What's more, feeding your baby her milk will remain an important source of comfort and will help to continue the bonding process. Your baby will need breast milk or formula until she is at least 12 months old, when her diet is varied enough to offer the correct balance of

> " *Weaning is a gentle process, involving slowly and sensitively replacing your baby's regular milk with healthy, delicious, nutritious food.* "

PREMATURE BABIES

Babies born before 37 weeks will have fewer nutritional stores than full-term babies. Breastfed premature babies will require a multivitamin that contains high levels of vitamin D and an iron supplement. Some mums will also be given a supply of breast milk fortifier to enrich their breast milk. Bottle-fed premature babies will be given prescription milk fortified with vitamins and iron. A dietitian will advise when to switch to regular formula.

If your baby was born prematurely, start weaning her between 5–8 months from the birth, but not before three months after the due date. This is to ensure she is developmentally ready to digest solids, while at the same time balancing the need for more nutrients. As with all babies, look for signs of developmental readiness (see page 30). Premature babies should be regularly reviewed by a Registered Dietitian who is qualified in children's nutrition.

nutrients. Breastfeeding can be successfully continued alongside the introduction of solid food. There is plenty of research to suggest that breast milk continues to offer antibodies well into toddlerhood, which can help your little one resist infection. It also contains a readily absorbed form of iron, as well as protein, essential fatty acids, vitamins, minerals, and enzymes, making it a perfect complement to a healthy, varied diet.

Breastfeed your baby as usual, or, if she is on formula milk, make sure she gets at least 600ml (1 pint) per day. Most parents find it easiest to continue with the morning and evening feeds and fit the other milk feeds around mealtimes, gradually giving a little less as their baby takes more solids. Feed your baby after her first tastes instead of before, so that she is hungrier and more willing to try foods on offer. Top her up with a milk feed once she's had a few spoonfuls of purée or rice.

Introducing a mixed diet

When you begin to wean your baby, you'll be introducing her to new tastes and textures. At the outset, she'll take these in the form of a liquid purée so that it's similar to her milk – it should be almost the same consistency as yogurt – and then progress to lumpier, thicker purées, then chopped or lightly mashed. In baby-led weaning (see page 34), you'll be introducing soft finger foods.

Variety is the order of the day. Introduce your baby to new foods (including those you may not usually have yourself!) every day or so. The greater the variety, the easier it will be to progress to a healthy, nutritious diet. Small amounts represent success in the early days, so don't panic if she doesn't manage a whole bowl.

The first stage is about introducing new tastes and textures and teaching the art of eating. If she doesn't like what's on offer, put it aside and try again another day.

TOP TIPS
Before you wean your baby, it's helpful to be aware of the top tips for successful weaning:

● Make sure your baby is ready. Pushing a young, reluctant baby will make the start of weaning upsetting for you both.
● Babies sometimes find the process a little clinical and become upset when mealtimes no longer involve the comfort of sucking milk. When offering your baby her very first taste or two you may find it easier to hold her on your lap, as this will help her feel loved and secure.
● When babies feed from the breast or a bottle they instinctively push their tongue forwards. Now your baby needs to learn to keep her tongue at the back of her mouth. If she can't get on with a spoon, try dipping a clean finger in the purée and let her suck your finger for the first few mouthfuls.
● Avoid feeding your baby when she's tired, irritable, or very hungry.
● Don't get hung up about portion sizes. If she's taking a little, you've done well.
● Don't compare your baby with others. She will develop at her own pace and it is no reflection on her intelligence or abilities.

WEANING TRUTHS AND MYTHS

The process of weaning is surrounded by myths. We've got grandma telling us that babies need to be weaned at three or four months in order to sleep through the night, then reports suggesting we're giving babies a lifetime of health problems if we do it sooner than six months. So what is the truth?

Sleeping through

Many babies continue to wake up at night, which can be exhausting for parents. If this is the case with your little one, once the weaning process is underway make sure you give him a nutritious evening meal that contains a carbohydrate, a protein, and a vegetable. Protein, in particular, takes a long time to digest and may help to keep your child satisfied for a longer period of time if he is waking up due to hunger.

Teething and weaning

The development of teeth doesn't mean your baby is ready for solids. Some babies cut their first milk teeth around four months, which is early for weaning, while others show no signs of teething until well after six months.

Weight gain

It's often suggested that underweight babies benefit from early weaning; however, research shows that continuing with milk feeds encourages your baby to reach his optimum weight as initial foods (fruit and vegetables) are often low in energy.

Weaning and food allergies

The previous advice was to delay introducing allergenic foods to reduce the risk of allergy. There is now excellent evidence that introducing eggs and peanuts from six months may reduce the risk of these food allergies.

In 2015, doctors at King's College, London, found that children with a history of eczema who ate products containing peanuts from the ages of four and 11 months had a 70 per cent reduced risk of developing an allergy to peanuts compared with children who ate them for the first time when they were older. However, if there is a high risk of food allergy (see page 20), get your baby allergy tested before you do this.

Avoiding wheat, meat, and dairy

Cutting out whole food groups is dangerous. Dairy is an important source of calcium, vital for teeth and bone growth. It's also a good source of protein. Wheat is a source of gluten, which can cause problems in a minority of babies (see page 23), but it is also a great source of carbohydrates, B vitamins, and fibre. After six months, it's a healthy addition to your baby's diet. As for meat, there are few other such readily available sources of easily absorbed iron.

Undigested foods

Check your baby's nappy for foods that come out whole – for example, peas and sweetcorn. This is a sign your baby is not developmentally ready for these foods, so you need to help by chopping, mashing, or puréeing them so that the nutrients are more accessible to his body. Passing food through the digestive system is hard work and undigested foods use up energy without providing any benefit to your baby.

Sally and Tom, 6 months

I put off weaning Tom for a week because I couldn't bear the thought of him taking that first big step towards independence. Although it seems silly now, I felt emotional at the thought that he would no longer be solely dependent on me. I love breastfeeding, and we both found it hugely comforting. Solid food seemed so clinical and it was a big reminder that our lovely feeds would at some point end.

I was also a bit nervous about giving him the right foods – I'm really keen on giving Tom the best start in life and making sure he's getting all the nutrients he needs to be strong and healthy. But in the end weaning was a huge success and he eagerly took to his first tastes. For our first purée, I chose organic sweet potatoes with a little expressed breast milk. At least I know he's getting the best there is!

CRITICAL NUTRIENTS

As the process of weaning usually starts at around six months, it is no longer recommended that foods are introduced singly (this advice is from a time when weaning began at four months) – and giving only fruit and vegetables won't provide your baby with the critical nutrients she needs. At six months of age, it is essential to wean your baby onto a varied diet.

Breast or formula milk still supplies a lot of your baby's nutritional needs, but it's not enough for the rapid growth and brain development that occurs between now and two years of age. So what are the critical nutrients your baby needs?

Iron

Most babies are born with enough iron stored to last around six months, which is helpful as breast milk contains only a small amount of iron and the iron supplement in formula milk isn't easily absorbed. From when your baby is four months old, her body begins to use iron stores quickly due to the start of a big growth spurt. The iron is used to fuel growth and make more

Iron-rich food. Lentils are a good source of iron and can easily be combined with nutritious vegetables.

haemoglobin in her blood, which carries oxygen to the brain, where it's needed for rapid brain development, including for intelligence.

From six months to two years, babies need more iron than at any other time in their lives. Babies who don't get enough can have sensory and cognitive impairment and it may affect their motor development. Built-in iron stores are depleted by six months – or even earlier if you were iron-deficient when pregnant or your baby had a low birth weight, so iron has to come from food. It's therefore essential to give iron-rich foods at least twice a day from six months. The best sources are red meat and dark poultry meat. Other iron-rich foods are fortified breakfast cereals; wholegrain cereal products, such as pasta; egg yolk; pulses, such as lentils; tofu; dark leafy green vegetables, such as kale; and dried fruit, such as apricots and dates. Try to pair non-meat iron-rich foods with vitamin C foods as they help iron absorption.

Fats

Despite their bad press for adults, high-fat foods are good for babies and toddlers so don't be afraid to give them. If your baby likes fruit, serve it with full-fat yogurt and toss vegetables in melted butter. Around 50 per cent of a baby's energy needs to come from fats and oils for growth and development, and a lack of fat can affect cognitive development. It won't be easy

Snack time. By giving healthy snacks as part of weaning, your baby will get a good intake of critical nutrients.

FIBRE

There are two types of fibre, but only one is good for your baby. Insoluble fibre, found in foods such as bran flakes, can't be digested and should be avoided. It sweeps food through your baby's digestive system quickly, which can make it difficult for her body to absorb important minerals. The other type is soluble fibre, which can be digested and is good for a healthy heart. It's found in oats, beans, pulses, vegetables, fruits, including dried, and wholegrain bread. Too much, however, can be filling and affect your baby's appetite. It can also cause tummy aches and loose stools, so use a combination of white and wholegrain bread, rice, pasta, and grains.

to get this much fat into your baby's diet because she may not eat much. Therefore it's important to choose energy-dense foods, such as whole or full-fat versions of milk, cream, yogurt, and cheese and cook with oil whenever you can. The best oils are rapeseed and olive – high in monounsaturated fatty acids, they are good for a healthy heart.

Protein

This is the main nutrient for growth, but it can't be used efficiently by the body unless your baby has enough energy (see page 14). Protein-rich foods include fish, meat, milk, cheese, nuts, eggs, beans, soya, and pulses.

Essential fatty acids (EFAs)

EFAs can't be made by the body so have to come from food. The most important one for babies is Docosahexaenoic acid (DHA), an omega-3 fatty acid, which is essential for brain development and the development of the retina. The only decent food source is oily fish, such as salmon, mackerel, sardines, pilchards, and fresh tuna (not canned), but don't give your baby oily fish more than twice a week as it can contain pollutants. DHA can also be found in eggs from hens fed with omega-3-rich grains, and it does pass through breast milk. A baby won't be able to meet her DHA requirements from vegetarian sources, such as walnuts and flaxseeds.

Fruit purées. These are a good source of vitamins, but from six months your baby needs a more varied diet to ensure an adequate intake of critical nutrients.

Carbohydrates

These are also energy providers and, alongside fats, provide the fuel required by your baby's body to make the best use of protein foods. Include a mixture of both white and wholegrain versions of grains, rice, bread, and pasta. Potatoes, sweet potatoes, and fortified breakfast cereals are also good sources.

Zinc

High-protein foods (see opposite) are the best source of zinc and are recommended from the outset of weaning. Zinc is needed for the development of a healthy immune system and a diet high in zinc helps to boost your baby's immunity. All of the iron-rich foods (see page 14) are also high in zinc, so if your baby has iron twice a day she'll also be getting enough zinc.

Vitamin D

This vitamin, made by the body when sunlight shines on the skin, is important for bone growth and essential for developing your baby's immune system. Oily fish, egg yolk, and fortified foods, such as some margarines, milks, and cereals, are the only food sources we have, so your baby won't be able to consume enough.

Therefore the recommendation is to give an 8.5–10mcg supplement daily. Infant formula already contains the supplement, but breastfed babies should receive drops (some families can get free drops from their health visitor). Most drops also contain vitamins A and C.

Exposing your baby's skin to sun is the best way to get vitamin D, but in the UK we don't get enough sun during winter.

Vitamin C

This is essential for iron absorption, healing, healthy skin and bones, and to boost immunity. All fruit and vegetables are good sources, but especially berries, papaya, mango, citrus fruit, kiwi fruit, broccoli, cauliflower, and sweet peppers.

FIRST TASTES

Your baby's first tastes are not intended to provide every known nutrient. However, because babies have small tummies, everything you serve should go some way towards helping her become strong and healthy. Babies also have fewer nutrient stores to draw from, which means that a balanced nutritional intake is important. What's more, likes and dislikes are established early, so helping your baby to develop a taste for healthy foods now will make mealtimes a lot easier in years to come.

When you first introduce your baby to solid foods, portion sizes aren't important. A few spoonfuls, once a day, will give her a taste of different flavours and provide a little nutrition. In time, your baby will probably begin to eat one or two "meals" a day. "Meals" can, however, be comprised of a very small amount of food.

You'll find your baby will let you know how much she needs to eat; some foods, such as carbohydrates, will fill her more quickly than fresh fruit and vegetables. When she appears to be full, or resists your attempts to feed her, it's a good idea to stop.

By the time your baby is on three meals a day and has cut down on her milk feeds (around 10 months), she needs to be eating plenty of fresh fruits and vegetables, good sources of protein, healthy fats, and good-quality carbohydrates to keep her diet balanced, her body healthy, and her energy levels high. Look at her diet across the day – as long as she is getting a little of each (ideally some carbohydrate, protein, and vegetable or fruit at every meal), you are doing well.

Critical Nutrients

SPECIAL DIETS

Whether you've chosen to remove certain foods from your baby's diet on health, religious, environmental, or ethical grounds, or his diet has to be restricted for other reasons, it's important to make sure that you make up for any shortfalls to guarantee he's getting all the nutrients he needs.

Vegetarian babies

The good news is that for the first six months of your baby's life, he will get most of the vitamins, minerals, and other nutrients he needs from his regular milk. Babies weaned before six months, start off vegetarian anyway, as fruit and vegetable purées form the basis of their diets for the first month or so. Around six months is when you introduce meat, poultry, and fish, so at this time you will need to look for alternative sources of iron, protein, zinc, and vitamin B_{12} for your vegetarian baby. Vitamin B_{12} is needed for healthy red blood cells, your baby's nervous system, and healthy growth and development and you can find it in eggs and dairy produce. A shortfall can lead to anaemia.

Offering dairy produce, pulses such as lentils, fortified cereals and other grains, leafy green vegetables and fruit, including dried fruit, should help to make sure your baby gets the nutrients that he needs. Provided there is no family history of allergy (see page 20), you can introduce peanut butter at this stage too. Include plenty of vegetarian sources of EFAs (see page 16), but as these are unlikely to meet his requirements, it may be necessary to top him up with a supplement.

Be aware that an adult vegetarian diet can be high in fibre, which is unsuitable for babies. High-fibre diets hinder iron absorption and are low in calories as well as essential fats, which may affect growth. If your baby is being brought up on a vegetarian diet, it's important to include nutrient-dense foods such as cheese, eggs, nut butters, and full-fat dairy products, as these will provide the extra nutrients required for healthy growth and development.

Vegan babies

If you're bringing your baby up as vegan, seek advice from a Registered Dietitian with expertise in children's nutrition. With careful planning, it is possible to meet his nutritional needs, as long as you always provide the critical nutrients (see pages 14–17). For protein: lentils, peas, beans, soya, yogurt, and nut butters. For carbohydrates: potatoes, sweet potatoes, grains, pasta, and bread. For fats: olive oil, rapeseed, and sunflower oil. For iron: wholegrain carbohydrates, plus peas, beans, lentils, nut butters, dried fruit, and tofu. Unfortunately, many fortified breakfast cereals are processed in factories that handle milk and therefore can't be labelled vegan. Vitamin C-rich foods such as fruit help iron absorption.

Vegan babies may not receive adequate zinc, as phytates in food decrease absorption, and iodine can also be in short supply – a supplement may be required. Vitamin B_{12} is found almost exclusively in animal products and so a vegan baby will only get this from breast milk (infant formula milks are not vegan).

Vitamins and other supplements

At six months, your baby's iron stores start to become depleted and your breast milk does not provide sufficient amounts, so it is important to progress with weaning foods that are nutrient-rich and contain iron (see page 14). All breastfed babies older than six months should be given a multivitamin containing vitamin A, C, and D.

Feeding a sick baby

When your baby is sick, follow your instincts: if he is hungry, offer him something to eat. If he shows an interest in food, stick to baby rice, and ripe apples and bananas – these place no pressure on the digestive system, but offer a little nutrition and energy. If he is not interested in solids, offer his usual milk feeds to keep him hydrated. Bottle-fed babies may require a little extra cooled boiled water, too. If he is off his milk, seek advice from a doctor who may recommend an oral rehydration solution. Most illnesses shift in 24 to 48 hours, but if your baby is floppy or listless with few wet nappies (signs of dehydration), see a doctor immediately.

Weight worries

Breastfeeding is the most effective way to prevent a baby becoming overweight, and breastfed babies are much less likely to develop problems with obesity in later life. If you are bottlefeeding, watch how and when you feed your baby. Don't be tempted to make him finish the bottle. Look for cues that he is full, and then stop. Babies under six months old don't usually need more than 600ml (1 pint) of milk per day. Similarly, when you start introducing solids, try to avoid over-feeding him – offer tastes, and when he loses interest stop.

If your baby is underweight, make sure he's getting enough milk and allow him to eat as much as he likes. Give a source of protein at every meal and include healthy fats (see pages 14–16) by stirring them into purées.

JENNY ASKS . . .

We plan to bring up our baby daughter as a vegetarian, but she doesn't seem to have much energy and I'm worried that her limited diet might be making her ill.

The most important thing to consider is whether your baby is getting an adequate balance of the critical nutrients (see pages 14–17).

An adequate intake of protein and iron can be difficult to achieve in a vegetarian diet. You should include iron-rich foods two to three times a day and pair them with vitamin-C-rich food, such as fresh fruit (preferably give this after your baby's meal so she isn't too full).

Your baby should have a protein food at each meal. Good protein foods are dairy foods such as cheese, milk, and yogurt, as well as beans, pulses, and tofu. You can give your baby unflavoured Quorn products but avoid giving her processed meat alternatives.

If nothing seems to make a difference to your baby's energy levels, talk to your doctor, who will investigate this further.

Special Diets

ALLERGY CONCERNS

Childhood food allergies seem to be on the increase, so it's not surprising that parents are nervous about introducing foods that could cause problems. Assessing whether your baby may be at risk, and learning to recognize the signs of food allergies, can help make weaning safe and successful.

What are allergies?

A food allergy is when the immune system has an adverse reaction to a usually harmless protein, leading to the release of histamine and other chemicals that cause symptoms such as itching and swelling. Symptoms usually occur a few minutes after eating. Food allergies affect only 5–6 per cent of young children.

Specific food allergies aren't inherited, but a tendency to get allergies like hay fever, asthma, and eczema, known as atopy, is inherited from one or both parents. It is more common to be atopic if both parents have this tendency. To help reduce the risk of allergies, it is best to breastfeed exclusively for six months, and there is emerging evidence to suggest that introducing foods like egg and peanut from six months may protect a child from developing allergies (see page 12).

Top food allergies

The most common food allergens in the UK are shown in the chart opposite. These must be clearly mentioned on food labels and menus when used as ingredients.

Although rare, the most common fruit allergy is to kiwi fruit. Some children with eczema may get a rash around their mouth when eating acidic fruit such as strawberries, but this can simply be a skin irritation. Rubbing some petroleum jelly around your baby's mouth will protect her skin.

Egg allergy

Being allergic to eggs is much more common in young children than in adults, but most children will outgrow it. However, children with egg allergy are also at a high risk of getting peanut and other allergies, so they should be seen by a doctor experienced in childhood allergies. Egg allergy can be to all forms of egg, but many people with egg allergy can eat baked foods containing well-cooked egg. Research has found that 70–80 per cent of children with an egg allergy can eat cakes and biscuits that contain egg, but in those allergic even to well-cooked egg the reactions can be severe.

A child with an egg allergy should be tested by an experienced doctor before eating foods containing egg. This may need to be done under direct medical supervision.

Egg replacement. Mashed banana can be used to replace egg in baking for those who have an allergy.

THE TOP FOOD ALLERGENS IN THE UK

Cow's milk
Milk is a common ingredient in butter, cheese, cream, milk powders, and yogurt. It can also be found in foods brushed or glazed with milk, and in powdered soups and sauces.

Tree nuts
Not to be mistaken with peanuts (which are actually a legume and grown underground), this refers to nuts that grow on trees, such as cashew nuts, almonds, and hazelnuts. It is very common for foods to contain nuts.

Chicken eggs
Eggs are often found in cakes, some meat products, mayonnaise, pasta, quiche, sauces, and foods brushed or glazed with egg.

Sesame
Sesame seeds can be often found in bread, breadsticks, hummus, sesame oil, and tahini. They are sometimes toasted and used in salads.

Shellfish
In particular, prawns, but also crab, lobster, and scampi.

Celery
Celery is often an ingredient in salads, soups, stuffings, and stock cubes.

Fish
Allergic reactions have been commonly reported to everything from anchovies to cod, and salmon to pollock. You might also find unexpected sources of fish in salad dressings, fish sauces, relishes, and Worcestershire sauce.

Kiwi fruit
Although it is rare, the most common fruit allergy in the UK is to kiwi fruit.

Soya
Soya is a staple ingredient in oriental food. It can also be found in bread, desserts, ice cream, meat products, sauces, and vegetarian foods.

Peanuts
Peanuts are often used as an ingredient in cereal bars and oriental foods and, of course, found in peanut butter.

Wheat
Wheat is often found in flour, baking powder, batter, breadcrumbs, bread, cakes, couscous, pasta, pastry, sauces, soups, and fried foods.

Molluscs
These include mussels, oysters, snails, squids, and whelks. They are commonly found as an ingredient in fish stews.

Allergy Concerns

Egg substitutes

In baking, eggs can be replaced with:

- 50g (1³/₄oz) apple purée
- 1 small mashed banana
- 50ml (1³/₄fl oz) custard (custard powder and milk plus 1¹/₄ teaspoons of baking powder)
- 1 tablespoon of arrowroot powder and half a teaspoon of baking powder
- An additional 15g (¹/₂oz) butter and a tablespoon of water for each egg in pastry
- Self-raising flour instead of plain and 50ml (1³/₄fl oz) milk for each egg in biscuits.

To replace eggs as a binder:

- Buttermilk
- Cornflour with sparkling water
- Chia seeds or flaxseeds mixed with water – a tablespoon of seeds to 3 tablespoons of water
- Aquafaba, which is tinned chickpea liquid: a tablespoon for one egg yolk and 2 tablespoons for one egg white – this can be used to make pancakes and meringues.

Nut allergy

About one in 50 children in the UK has a nut allergy. A child has a higher risk of developing a peanut allergy if she already has an allergic condition, such as eczema or a diagnosed food allergy, or if there is a family history of atopy, such as asthma or hay fever. Peanuts, peanut products, and tree nuts can induce a severe allergic reaction (see box, opposite), so be cautious if there is a history of allergy.

The advice on giving nuts has changed: for babies where there are no allergy concerns, peanut butter and finely ground nuts can be introduced from six months. The advice used to be that a child allergic to peanuts should avoid nuts completely. However, there is concern that many children who do this may develop an allergy to nuts they were not allergic to because they avoided eating them at a critical time.

Tree nuts, such as cashews, pecans, walnuts, pistachio, and almonds, are not related to peanuts but can also cause reactions. You may be advised not to give other nuts to your child if your child is allergic to peanuts. Whole nuts should be avoided until five years of age due to the risk of choking.

Cow's milk allergy

Cow's milk protein allergy (CMPA) is one of the most common childhood food allergies, estimated to affect 2–7.5 per cent of babies aged under one. Most children grow out of it by the age of five. CMPA typically develops when cow's milk is first introduced. More rarely, it can affect babies who are exclusively breastfed, because of cow's milk protein being passed on through breast milk so you may be advised to remove all cow's milk from your diet. It will not help to switch to lactose-free products as these still contain cow's milk protein.

CMPA can cause symptoms such as eczema, wheezing, vomiting, diarrhoea, constipation, hives, and/or a stuffy, itchy nose. Occasionally, it can cause anaphylaxis (see box, opposite). If your baby is diagnosed with CMPA, your GP or an allergy specialist will refer you to a Registered Dietitian.

Nut allergy. It is now believed that delaying giving nuts can, in fact, increase the risk of an allergy developing.

Cow's milk substitute formulas

Infant formula is made from cow's milk, so if your baby has a cow's milk allergy, this will need to be replaced with a special formula.

● Extensively hydrolysed formulas and amino acid-based formulas prescribed upon recommendation by a Registered Dietitian.

● Soya-based infant formula, but these are not recommended for babies under six months because of concerns about plant oestrogen levels. Also around 20 per cent of babies who are allergic to milk are also allergic to soya because the proteins appear very similar to a baby's immune system.

Note: Partially hydrolysed formulas (available without prescription), where proteins are broken down to make them less allergenic, are not suitable for babies with CMPA.

Always consult your GP or a Registered Dietitian with experience in children's nutrition to determine which formula is best for your baby. Early diagnosis is important because these types of formula don't taste good, but the earlier you introduce them, the more likely they are to be accepted by your baby. The dietitian will be able to suggest techniques for helping your baby transition to the new milk.

In the first year, babies will need at least 500–600ml (16fl oz–1 pint) of hypoallergenic formula per day in order to meet their nutritional requirements.

Alternative milks for older children

● Oat milk and milks made from foods such as nuts, soya, hemp, or coconut will not provide adequate nutrients for children under five, but can be used in cooking in place of cow's milk.

● Older children can have the milks listed above, but will need advice from a dietitian on replacing missing nutrients as these milks are low in protein, energy, vitamins, and minerals.

● Rice milk is not recommended for children under four-and-a-half years old due to high

> ## ANAPHYLAXIS
>
> If your baby has symptoms that affect her breathing, call an ambulance immediately or go to your local A&E department. This is an anaphylactic reaction, which can cause a drop in blood pressure known as "shock". Symptoms include breathing problems, sudden pallor, inexplicable and sudden drowsiness, facial swelling, and possibly even collapse.

levels of naturally occurring arsenic, although rice products such as rice cake or rice pudding are fine.

Note: Sheep's, goat's, and other animal milks are not suitable alternatives for babies who are allergic to cow's milk protein as their immune systems are unable to distinguish between the protein sources – these milks will cause the same reaction as cow's milk.

If your child is fussy about having alternative milks, you will need to seek guidance from a Registered Dietitian with experience in children's nutrition to ensure your child is getting the critical nutrients she needs.

Milk ladder

Babies aged over nine months who have a mild form of milk allergy may undergo a milk challenge after following a cow's milk-free diet for a full six months.

A "milk ladder" is used to gradually introduce the milk under the supervision of a Registered Dietitian, starting with highly baked forms of cow's milk incorporated with certain carbohydrates and fats. If your baby is able to tolerate cooked forms of milk, she should have them routinely in her diet, in order to receive a little more calcium and other nutrients.

Wheat allergy and coeliac disease

A wheat allergy is uncommon and usually found in children who have eczema or multiple food allergies. It is usually outgrown in childhood.

Coeliac disease, which often runs in families, is different to a wheat allergy as it is an auto-immune condition triggered by a protein called gluten in certain grains (wheat, rye, barley). Symptoms include chronic diarrhoea, tiredness, tummy ache, iron deficiency, faltering growth, and offensive-smelling poo. It is diagnosed by a blood test and endoscopy, but your child needs to be having wheat in her diet when tested so always see the doctor before you cut it out entirely. Unfortunately, gluten can be hidden in food such as soups, sauces, fish fingers, chicken nuggets, and salad dressings.

It's important not to cut wheat or gluten out of your child's diet unnecessarily as she may then be at risk of developing deficiencies in energy, B vitamins, and fibre.

When looking for wheat alternatives, it is vitally important to check the labelling on packaging. Gluten-free doesn't mean wheat-free. Sometimes a product may contain the rest of the wheat grain with just the gluten removed.

People with coeliac disease can only eat foods labelled as "gluten-free" as even traces of gluten can cause problems. If your child has coeliac disease, check food labels carefully or use the Coeliac UK food scanner app to. Don't just assume the food is safe as many naturally gluten-free foods can be cross-contaminated.

Wheat substitutes

- You can substitute wheat-free and gluten-free flours for plain flour. However, it is generally best to substitute where there is a low ratio of flour to other ingredients as then you are less reliant on gluten to hold the mixture together. Always grease and line cake tins well – gluten-free baked products tend to be more fragile.
- When you are baking, use Xanthan gum with gluten-free flour to enhance the texture so that the finished product is less crumbly.
- Crushed corn flakes or rice krispies make a good coating for home-made fish fingers or chicken nuggets, but not all are gluten-free so do check carefully.
- Gluten-free panko (Japanese) breadcrumbs.
- Rice flour, polenta, buckwheat, cornflour, arrowroot, and potato flour are all naturally gluten-free so are suitable for coeliacs.
- Rice noodles are a good substitute for pasta.
- Quinoa, millet, tapioca, amaranth, and rice are good alternatives to grains.
- There are many gluten-free and wheat-free breads, crackers, pasta, and pizza bases available in supermarkets.
- Cornflour and soya flour.
- Ground almonds work well in biscuits, cakes, breads, and doughs.

Note: Oats are now allowed in gluten-free diets as it is recognized that oat gluten is different to wheat, rye, and barley gluten. However, people with coeliac disease should buy gluten-free oats to avoid those that may have been contaminated by gluten during processing.

KEEPING A FOOD DIARY

A good way to pinpoint problem foods is to make a note of every food you introduce, and any reactions your baby has. Even if your baby doesn't suffer from allergies, it can be useful to record details of foods she has tried. If you have allergies in the family, it is advisable to wait 48 hours between the introduction of the potentially allergenic foods to see if there is a reaction. So, try dairy produce, for example, and then wait for two days before introducing eggs. It is a good idea to introduce new foods at breakfast or lunchtime, so you can monitor your baby's reaction during the day.

FREQUENTLY ASKED QUESTIONS

Here I've addressed some of the most common questions parents ask me.

Q *My husband and I have food allergies. Will my son develop them?*
A No, but there is a good chance he will inherit an allergic tendency, which means he could develop eczema or asthma or an allergy to something else. A tendency to get allergies and allergic problems, such as hay fever, asthma, and eczema, is known as atopy. It is more common to be atopic if both parents have this tendency. However, specific allergies are not inherited.

Q *How can I protect my baby daughter from potential food allergies?*
A The best thing you can do is breastfeed exclusively for 4–6 months. There is also emerging evidence that introducing weaning foods, especially eggs and peanuts, from six months may protect against developing allergies to these foods. Avoiding particular foods during pregnancy or breastfeeding does not seem to make any difference to the likelihood of allergies.

Q *Does delaying giving certain foods reduce the development of allergies?*
A It is now known that delaying the introduction of allergenic foods, such as milk, eggs, and peanuts is not helpful and can lead to a higher risk of developing a food allergy. However, if your baby has a high risk of allergy, for example she has severe eczema or there's a strong family history, then get her allergy tested.

Q *How much time should I leave between introducing each new food ?*
A As reactions usually happen very soon after exposure, there is no need to leave long gaps. Just introduce one allergenic food at a time,

Breastfeeding. Breast milk has many health benefits for babies, one of which is that it may help to prevent them from developing food allergies.

leaving 48 hours in between each. It is important not to delay the introduction of allergenic foods as this may increase the chance of an allergy developing.

Q *How do I know if my daughter has an allergy or an intolerance?*
A There are two sorts of allergy: immediate-onset allergies occur within minutes of the food being eaten. Delayed-onset allergies are more likely to cause your baby to have eczema, reflux, colic, or diarrhoea. Intolerances are an entirely different condition, but can be just as upsetting. If your baby is suffering from any unusual symptoms after eating particular foods, it's important that you take her to see your doctor and meanwhile withhold the offending food. If you are unable to identify the offending food you can ask

for a referral to a Registered Dietitian with expertise in children's nutrition, who can guide you through an elimination diet.

Q *How much of an allergen is needed to trigger an allergic response?*
A Immediate-onset allergies can be caused by a very small exposure to an allergen, although severe reactions will not happen unless the food is eaten. Contact with the skin will only cause minor reactions. With delayed-onset reactions, where a food such as milk or soya causes chronic symptoms such as eczema, reflux, or colic, it will be worse the more of the allergen that is consumed.

Q *How do I arrange for my daughter to have an allergy test?*
If you are concerned about food allergies your GP can organize a referral for allergy testing at the children's unit of your local hospital. Don't buy allergy tests from the internet as these are unreliable and often lead to misdiagnosis. Allergy tests can be arranged privately if there is a long waiting list – again your GP will refer you.

Q *How do I arrange for my child to see a Registered Dietitian?*
Your GP can make a referral to an NHS Registered Dietitian with expertise in Children's Nutrition. You can also self-refer to a private practice Registered Dietitian. It's important to find one who has expertise in Children's Nutrition.

Q *If my baby is allergic to one food, is she likely to have other food allergies?*
A No, having one food allergy will not increase the risk of having further food allergies. However, certain allergies often go together such as milk and soya, and peanut and tree nuts.

Q *Will my baby outgrow his allergy?*
A Fortunately, allergies to milk, egg, soya, and wheat are usually outgrown during childhood, while allergies to peanut, tree nuts, fish, and shellfish tend to persist into adulthood.

Q *My son has a severe peanut allergy. Will my baby daughter also get it?*
A There is a 7 per cent risk of a sibling of a child with peanut allergy also becoming allergic. Consider getting your daughter tested just before weaning so that if the test is negative, peanut can be introduced into the diet, to reduce the risk of an allergy to it developing.

Q *What are the links between asthma, eczema, and allergies?*
A These are all atopic diseases, meaning that they are all related to allergies. Children who are atopic (the inherited tendency to get allergies) often go through the "allergic march"– a progression of conditions. This usually starts with eczema in infancy, which predisposes to getting food allergies. Both these conditions often improve, but give way to respiratory allergy including asthma and hay fever.

Q *My son is allergic to dairy. When can I start to re-introduce cow's milk?*
A This is dependent upon the symptoms. It will be decided by a Registered Dietitian who works to official guidelines managing milk allergy.

> "
> *It is important not to delay the introduction of allergenic foods as this may increase the chance of an allergy developing.*
> "

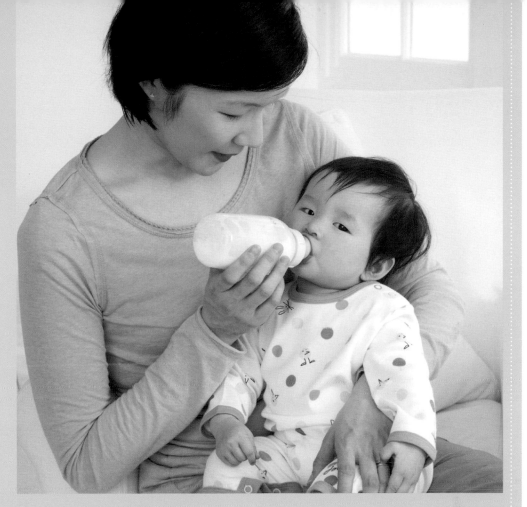

Milk allergy. Children usually outgrow an allergy to cow's milk, but it should only be reintroduced under the supervision of a Registered Dietitian.

Q *I'm still breastfeeding. If my son has a food allergy, do I need to cut that food out of my diet?*

A If your baby is allergic to certain foods such as milk, egg, soya, or wheat, what you eat can sometimes pass via your breast milk into your son's diet, although it is rare. Rather than having an immediate reaction, there may be a delayed reaction, affecting the gut or a worsening of eczema, for example. You should seek advice before trying to cut any foods out of your own diet. For example, if you cut milk from your diet, you will need to include an alternative source of protein and calcium to make sure that your milk is providing enough calcium for your baby. In this instance I would suggest seeing a Registered Dietitian with expertise in children's nutrition.

Q *What is a food challenge?*

A Apart from a skin prick test or blood test, one of the best ways to diagnose a food allergy is a food challenge. The child is put on an elimination diet where the suspected food or foods are removed from the diet, then reintroduced under medical supervision and the child is watched for signs and symptoms of an allergic reaction.

REFLUX, CONSTIPATION, AND DIARRHOEA

Gastro-intestinal and bowel problems can be an unfortunate side-effect of many allergy-related conditions. Look out for the signs and symptoms and don't hesitate to seek advice from your doctor if you have any concerns.

Gastro-oesophageal reflux

Gastro-oesophageal reflux is a condition in which the stomach contents – food (milk) and acid – come back up into the oesophagus (food pipe) or into the mouth. This condition can sometimes be a sign of cow's milk protein allergy (see page 22).

Most babies have a degree of reflux because the muscular valve at the end of their oesophagus, which acts to keep food in the stomach, hasn't developed fully yet. This means that when your baby's stomach is full, milk can come back up. If he brings up small amounts of milk it's called possetting and this is normal. Babies often posset a bit when burping, hence the use of muslins over the shoulder.

During a baby's first year, the muscular valve gradually gets stronger and better at keeping food down, so the possetting reduces and the chance of having reflux decreases. It's only when strong acid from the baby's stomach comes up into his oesophagus that it can be painful and start to cause problems – this is called gastro-oesophageal reflux and is not that common.

Around 50 per cent of all babies will experience some reflux during their first three months, but this will prove to be a problem for only a very few and they will usually outgrow it. By the age of 10 months, the number of babies experiencing reflux will have dropped to around 5 per cent.

Symptoms of reflux

If your baby shows discomfort when feeding, such as arching his back, refusing to feed, and crying, it can be a sign of reflux. He may also frequently vomit or posset more than normal (possetting is only about a teaspoon) and cough a lot, including at night, with no other sign of a cold. Other symptoms include excessive regurgitation, weight loss or poor weight gain, and waking often. To alleviate the symptoms of reflux:

● Give small frequent feeds (6–7 feeds a day).
● Avoid the slump position, which adds pressure to the stomach – this can happen when a baby is seated in a bouncy chair or car seat.
● Try to keep your baby upright during feeding and for about 20 minutes after.
● In more severe cases, your doctor or health visitor may suggest adding infant Gaviscon to your baby's formula or expressed breast milk. Note that Infant Gaviscon is a completely different product to Gaviscon. Only use feed thickeners and thickened milk if advised to by your health visitor, dietitian, or doctor.

Constipation

Sometimes babies become constipated when they are first introduced to solids after being exclusively breastfed. It can also be caused by not eating enough fibre-rich foods such as vegetables, fruit, and wholegrain cereals or not drinking enough fluids. You can try to stimulate your baby's bowels by bicycling his legs around while he lies on his back or gently massaging his tummy. Foods that can help relieve constipation are those that contain soluble fibre (see page 16). Don't give bran or bran-containing products as this is insoluble fibre, which a baby's bowels are not mature enough to deal with.

Diarrhoea

Diarrhoea is when the poo is watery and offensive-smelling. In babies, frequent abnormal watery stools are often caused by a viral infection, gastroenteritis. If it persists see your GP as babies can become dehydrated very quickly. Signs of dehydration include a sunken soft spot (fontanelle) on a young baby's head, sunken eyes, dry mouth or lips, fewer wet nappies, dark yellow urine, and possible listlessness. Seek urgent medical help if you think your baby is dehydrated.

A fibre boost. Giving your baby foods rich in soluble fibre, such as fruit, can help to relieve constipation.

Never dilute your baby's formula, but you can offer sips of water between feeds. Breast milk has the optimum level of fluids and electrolytes needed to recover from diarrhoea, so breastfeed on demand. Keep your baby's diet bland with foods such as banana, dry toast, infant rice cereal, apple, potato, and pasta, until she is well again.

> " *Sometimes babies become constipated when they are first introduced to solids after being exclusively breastfed.* "

Dinner for one.
It will be easier
to wean your
baby on to solids
once he can sit
up unsupported
in his highchair.

IS YOUR BABY READY FOR WEANING?

Your baby needs to be developmentally ready to start weaning. The UK government guidelines recommend that weaning starts at around six months of age and that breast milk is nutritionally adequate for the first six months. By this time, your baby's digestive system and immune system are mature enough to digest solids and she is neurologically capable.

Note that actual age and developmental age are not the same thing. Babies develop at their own pace, which is why the words "around six months" are used. You as a parent are the best judge of when your baby is ready to wean, but never start before 17 weeks as your baby's digestive system isn't mature enough. Consult your GP or health visitor if you are in any doubt.

If your baby is showing signs of being ready after 17 weeks, you could try giving solids. The developmental signs of readiness are:
- Able to sit up with minimal support
- Tongue thrust has disappeared
- Can grab toys and put them into her mouth with good hand control
- Shows an interest in what you are eating.

Remember that sucking is a natural reflex, but swallowing and moving food around the mouth and from the front to the back needs to be learned. If you are doing baby-led weaning (see page 34), your baby needs to have sufficient hand-to-eye co-ordination to self-feed.

> *You as a parent are the best judge of when your baby is ready to start solids, but never start weaning before 17 weeks.*

Getting started

If you start weaning before six months, your baby is likely to still have some critical nutrients (see pages 14–17) stored, so start with simple fruit and vegetable purées to get her used to different tastes and textures. At this stage you can take your time introducing solids – you only need to step up the pace and variety of foods once your baby nears the six-month mark.

If you choose to start weaning closer to or at six months, you don't have the luxury of time. Still start with simple solids, but be mindful that within a week or two you need to start to offer more nutrient-rich foods that include the critical nutrients. Start with one meal a day, then if your baby seems eager to eat more introduce a second meal and then a third. If she gets frustrated with eating, give her a milk feed first so she's not overly hungry. Be guided by her cues – all babies are different.

Meal planning from six months

Once weaning is established, serve three foods at a time to make up a mini meal containing the critical nutrients:
- Start with an iron-rich protein food such as a scrambled egg or some slow-cooked beef.
- Add a vitamin C-rich fruit or vegetable, such as two raspberries or a steamed broccoli floret.
- Finish with an energy-dense carbohydrate food, such as a soldier of buttered toast.

Remember your baby needs iron-rich foods twice a day (see page 14).

If you're doing baby-led weaning (see page 34) or offering a combination of purées and finger food, your baby needs to be able to grasp food. She will use her whole fist to pick it up – the palm grip. At first, more of the food will be played with, squashed, or thrown on the floor, and that's fine; your baby is learning about the sensory characteristics of different foods.

Initially when offered foods she can feed herself, your baby will often just suck them rather than eat them, and this is fine, too. You will find that some foods are swallowed while others are carefully mouthed and spat out. That's okay – your baby is learning which foods she can swallow for the stage she's at. Persevere with these spat-out foods – eventually she'll swallow them when she's developmentally ready.

As weaning progresses

Notice when your baby starts to eat more food, which could be anytime from two to eight weeks after starting weaning – all babies are different.

New skills. Self-feeding simple finger foods, such as pieces of fruit, will develop your baby's hand-to-eye co-ordination and encourage independence.

If you're not sure how much your baby is eating, check the contents of her nappies. If the poo is still yellowish, she's still having a predominantly milk-based diet and is playing with her food. If the poo is browner, it's a sure sign she's eating!

Note also her ability to manage her own spoon – this can be pre-loaded by you and self-fed or she can dip the spoon into her own bowl and transfer it to her mouth. If she can do this, that's another milestone reached.

The pincer grip is another developmental milestone, where your baby can pick up and hold food between her thumb and index finger.

When these things happen, consider stepping up to mixed family meals instead of three separate items. Try recipes such as Beginner's Beef Casserole (see pages 114–15), Annabel's Tasty Pasta Bolognese (see page 148), and Chicken Quesadilla (see page 143).

As a guide, by the time your baby is eight months old, she will be having three meals a day of mixed family foods. By 10 months she should be having three meals a day and two snacks. Don't forget throughout this time your baby should still be receiving breast or formula milk on demand in between meal and snack times. Babies have very small stomachs so they need to eat more frequently than adults – they will need to eat something every 2½–3 hours.

Amount of food

There are no recommendations for portion sizes as all babies will eat different amounts. As a rule of thumb, once your baby is having three meals a day you could offer a tablespoon of each part of the meal – for example, meat, vegetables, and pasta – and let her eat the amount she wants. Signs of still being hungry can be an open mouth, reaching for more, sucking fists after finishing, or signing for more. If your baby doesn't seem hungry, avoid encouraging "just one more mouthful" as this can lead to an unhealthy relationship with food.

OFFERING NEW FOODS

Below is a guide to the foods that are appropriate for your baby's growth and development at each stage of weaning – some babies will be ready for a greater variety earlier than others.

AGE	FOODS	CONSISTENCY	ROUTINE
BETWEEN 17 WEEKS AND SIX MONTHS	• Fruits and vegetables such as ripe peaches, banana, mango, papaya, pear, melon, avocado, potato, swede, carrots, parsnip, sweet potato, and butternut squash. • Baby rice, porridge, cereals • Fats and oils	Thin, smooth purées	Introduce one meal a day initially and increase over the next few weeks so that by six months your baby is being offered three meals a day.
AT AROUND SIX MONTHS	As above	Thin, smooth purées	Limit to 1–2 weeks only. Progress from offering a meal a day to offering three meals per day in this 1–2 week period.
FROM SIX MONTHS	• Meat, poultry, fish, eggs • All fruit and vegetables • All cereal grains • All fats and oils	• Thicker purées or mashed foods • Well-cooked meat • Melt-in-the-mouth or bite-and-dissolve finger foods	Three meals – breakfast, lunch, dinner – with each meal consisting of an iron-rich food, an energy food, a fruit and vegetable. Give breast or formula milk on demand.
FROM AROUND EIGHT MONTHS	• Family foods – avoid salty, sugary foods – and don't give honey until aged 12 months. • Give meals rather than separate food items. See planner, page 121. • Small finger foods – e.g. peas and raisins – to practise pincer grip	• Finger food-based meals or chopped/roughly mashed meals. • Smaller finger foods	Continue to offer three meals per day. Give breast or formula milk on demand.
FROM AROUND 10 MONTHS	As eight months, plus two snacks in between meals. Good snacks are banana; yogurt; peanut butter on toast; cheese sticks; raisins; home-made cookie; boiled eggs; mini sandwiches; breadsticks and hummus; cheese scones; eggy bread; flapjack with milk.	As eight months, above	Offer three meals a day and two nutritious snacks between meals. Breakfast; mid-morning snack; lunch; mid-afternoon snack; dinner. Give breast or formula milk on demand.

BABY-LED WEANING

Lots of parents wean their babies by giving spoon-fed purées, but a different approach called baby-led weaning is growing evermore popular. This method forgoes purées and spoon-led feeding. Instead you simply let your baby feed himself. The ethos behind this method is that it gives a baby the chance to explore a variety of foods, tastes, and textures for himself.

In baby-led weaning a range of finger foods are offered to give the baby an element of choice, as well as soft food that the baby can spoon-feed himself. It is normal for babies to play with the food rather than eat it, but this is all part of their development. They will soon progress to sucking, chewing, and swallowing.

What are the benefits?

● It is believed that baby-led weaning helps a baby to develop healthy eating habits for life.
● Babies can explore a variety of foods, tastes, and textures for themselves, at their own pace.
● Babies can stop eating when they are full. Although most spoon-fed babies make it clear when they've had enough, parents often persist and some babies, eager to please, accept more.
● Babies learn to manage different food shapes and textures from the start, so they become skilled at handling a wide range of foods. This can help improve hand-to-eye co-ordination.
● It can simplify mealtimes as you give your baby foods from your meal and it encourages healthier eating for the whole family.
● Being seated at the table for meals with the rest of the family encourages social skills.

Are there any drawbacks?

● In baby-led weaning, babies can sometimes eat less than those who are spoon-fed and so are at a greater risk of receiving insufficient critical nutrients (see pages 14–17), which are required in the first 12 months. Insufficient iron, zinc, and vitamins are a worry, particularly for a breastfed baby as formula contains a multivitamin and mineral supplement but breast milk does not. This is where some form of puréeing or mashing of nutrient-rich food becomes important.
● Not all babies are developmentally ready for successful self-feeding, so it may be better to spoon-feed alongside giving soft finger foods. Some babies simply don't cope as well as others with starting solids and need a more gradual transition. For babies who are weaned earlier than six months, purées are a better bridge between milk and solids.

ACCEPTING THE MESS!

While your baby is experimenting with self-feeding, take a deep breath when things get messy. Fully exploring food is an important part of the sensory experience of eating for your baby – constantly cleaning his hands with wipes or spooning food from around his lips can hinder this important part of his development. Placing a mess mat or washable tablecloth under your baby's chair will allow you to recycle food that has been dropped. Invest in some large bibs with sleeves, too.

• A baby who was born prematurely is unlikely to be developmentally ready for baby-led weaning. If your baby was premature, seek advice from your Health Visitor or a Registered Dietitian.

Safety guidelines

• Never leave your baby alone while eating, and ensure he is supported in an upright position.
• Be careful about the textures you offer as some will be difficult for your baby to manage. At the start of weaning, finger foods should be able to be squashed between the finger and thumb.
• Avoid finger foods that your baby could break into large chunks, such as raw carrot, and small, round foods, such as cherry tomatoes, grapes, or giant blueberries. Halve, or even quarter, them.

Can I combine spoon-feeding with the principles of baby-led weaning?

Yes. Some parents feel a need to choose one method, but you don't have to. At around six months, you have the freedom to combine an element of baby-led weaning alongside spoon-feeding if you feel that's right for you and your baby. Some babies thrive on purées, others on

Favourite foods. Due to the element of choice with baby-led weaning, you may get a better sense of which foods your baby really likes.

finger foods and yet some on both. Instead of committing to a certain feeding method, it's okay to be flexible and to follow your intuition and your baby's developmental signs.

In speaking to parents, dietitians, nutritionists, and healthcare professionals about the various approaches to weaning, combining both methods is a popular option and one that many parents are finding the most realistic to adopt. Offering a mix of puréed foods as well as soft fingers foods at the beginning is also advocated by the Department of Health and the NHS and the British Nutrition Foundation. Both baby-led weaning and spoon-feeding allow your baby to explore a variety of different tastes, flavours, and textures.

However you decide to wean your baby, the important thing is to provide a variety of foods (particularly much-loved family foods) and allow your baby to go at his own pace.

First tastes

Stage One – around 6 months

Your baby's first tastes **mark a big milestone in his life** and can be exhilarating and nervewracking for you. Preparing equipment and ingredients in advance, **and getting to grips** with the best first foods can help make the process easier. The **best advice** is to take it slowly, spend time planning your baby's meals, and **go at his pace.** He'll soon get into the swing of things and enjoy **experimenting** with a variety of different tastes.

• *Menu planners pages 68–71*

GETTING STARTED: WHAT YOU'LL NEED

A little planning makes weaning your baby that much easier and you'll be surprised how little equipment you need to prepare nutritious, delicious first foods. You may already have most things you need to get started, and buying a few carefully chosen items will help to make mealtimes an enjoyable and positive experience for you and your baby.

● An electric hand-blender

This is great for making small quantities of baby food, and for puréeing family meals for your baby (you can freeze these in small portions and use them as you need them). A hand-blender is essential if you don't have a food processor. Look out for a model that has several speeds.

● A food processor

This is ideal for producing larger quantities of purées for freezing, and some also come with mini-bowl attachments for whizzing up small quantities when required. Choose a food processor with a variety of blades for creating textured foods later on.

● A masher

A potato-masher, or even a potato ricer (rather like a large garlic press), is perfect for creating lumpier textures. Look for a mini-masher, making it easy to mash and crush small amounts of food.

● An ice-cube tray

Freeze small portions of purée in ice-cube trays and tip out a portion or two to defrost when required. Choose a flexible tray with a lid. Perhaps consider buying several trays in different colours, which can help you to identify the contents.

Key
● **Essential**
○ **Useful**

● A high chair

Choose one that provides good support, including for your baby's feet. Small babies require a padded insert and a five-point harness is essential. High chairs that can be raised or lowered to allow sitting at the table are also useful. Some parents use Bumbo seats – these don't provide adequate support and as they are made to be placed on the floor, they aren't suitable for feeding.

● A flask

A wide-necked flask, which will keep food warm or cool for several hours, is ideal for transporting food for your baby. This can also be used to carry hot water, which can then be used for warming baby food. Look for a flask that can be used in the microwave and washed in the dishwasher.

● A bib

Babies are messy, no matter how careful you are. Plastic wipe-clean bibs are useful, as well as those with a curve at the base to collect food that doesn't make it to her mouth. Choose a bib that fits comfortably under your baby's chin. Younger babies may prefer soft, cotton ones.

● Feeding spoons

Choose a soft, plastic spoon that won't hurt your baby's gums. It should be small enough to fit easily into her mouth and have a long handle. Special weaning spoons are shallower – they are specifically designed for the developmental stages of weaning.

● Small bowls

To begin with you'll need small food containers that you can hold in one hand – these are ideal for freezing, storing, and re-heating food, and you can also feed your baby from them (see page 52). Choose ones with lids to make transportation easy, and make sure they are dishwasher safe.

● A lidded cup

From six months, milk and other drinks should be offered in a cup. Avoid the non-spill type as these require your baby to continue sucking rather than learning to drink. The liquid should flow freely, but not too quickly. Some brands have specific flow settings, which can be set according to your baby's age. Cups with soft, easy-to-grip handles are essential.

○ A steamer

Not only does this provide a quick and easy way to cook fruit, vegetables, fish, and poultry, but steaming also helps preserve essential nutrients, making sure your baby gets the most from what she eats.

○ A mouli (small food grinder)

A mouli is ideal for foods with tougher skins, such as peas or dried fruit, making it easier to separate the less digestible parts. It is also the best way to purée potato as using a food processor makes it go sticky.

○ A mess mat

Placed under your baby's chair, this mat will protect carpets and flooring from inevitable spills. Choose one that is non-slip, stain-resistant, and wipe-clean. Large mats are ideal, as your baby's firing range will undoubtedly increase as she gets older.

WHICH FOODS SHOULD I CHOOSE?

Your baby's food should be as fresh as possible, without any added ingredients, such as colourings, flavourings, salt, or sugar. Choosing fresh or frozen local produce will help you make sure he gets the nutrients he needs.

Fresh or frozen?

While fresh food would appear to be healthier for your baby, the truth is that a good proportion of the produce we eat has been picked well before its prime and has probably then sat in the back of a lorry or on a supermarket shelf for some time. If you can get fresh food from a greengrocer with a quick turnover or a farmers' market (or, indeed, grow it yourself), fresh is best. However, second best is most definitely frozen. Frozen food has been flash-frozen, often minutes after picking, and it maintains the highest level of nutrients.

Local and seasonal

Locally grown food spends less time being packaged and transported, and therefore contains a higher number of nutrients. Organic box schemes, farm shops, and farmers' markets are good sources, or you can grow your own. Most locally grown food will also be in season. Fruit and vegetables in season are less expensive, and also likely to be fresher and more nutritious.

Raw or cooked?

Ideally, raw fruits and vegetables contain a greater quantity as well as different types of nutrients than cooked. More than half the nutrients of raw foods are destroyed in the cooking process, depending on the way you cook them (see page 48). Raw foods contain enzymes that are required by the body to break down other foods, which helps us to absorb what we need from what we eat. Having said that, raw foods tend to be high in fibre, which is not ideal for little tummies. What's more, research shows that we absorb more nutrients from some cooked foods than we would if they were raw. Carrots and tomatoes are good examples. What's the answer? A few soft, raw, fresh foods (mangoes and bananas) make delicious and nutritious purées for babies. However, until weaning is established and they are eating regular meals, the majority of their food should be cooked.

GOING ORGANIC?

Although organic food, which is grown and processed without the use of artificial chemicals and potentially dangerous pesticides, has been proven to be better for the environment, there is little evidence to support claims that it is more nutritious. That said, some parents who make their own purées using organic ingredients believe that they have more natural sweetness and flavour, which helps when introducing babies to food. Be aware, however, that because of strict guidelines governing what can and can't be added to organic products, you won't find foods fortified with iron and calcium, which is important for growing babies.

BEST FIRST FOODS

A plain purée of a single fruit or root vegetable mixed with your baby's usual milk is the perfect first food. Your baby will be used to the sweet taste of milk, so choose fruit and sweeter varieties of vegetables to start.

It's fine to start with single fruit or vegetable purées. There's no evidence that giving fruits first hinders acceptance of vegetables. In fact, fruit is an integral part of successful weaning.

Baby rice

Mixed with water, breast milk, or formula, baby rice has a sweet, milky taste and is easily digested. It can be blended to almost any consistency, making it an ideal starter food. Choose a brand that is sugar-free and enriched with vitamins and iron and follow the instructions on the packet. Avoid gluten-containing cereals, such as wheat, rye, and barley, until your baby is at least six months old.

Millet

This gluten-free cereal is a good starter food for little ones and has a mild, sweet, nut-like flavour. It contains B vitamins, some vitamin E, and is particularly high in iron, which is important for growing babies. Millet blends well with your baby's usual milk and both fruit and vegetables. Simply follow the instructions on the packet.

Carrot

The sweet taste of carrots appeals to babies. Cook them until they are soft enough to purée (see page 62). Orange-coloured root vegetables are rich in

FIRST TASTES // Stage One – around 6 months

baby rice

millet

carrot

Don't put too much on the spoon

Colourful food equals plenty of nutrients

beta-carotene, which is essential for your baby's growth, healthy skin, and good vision.

Potato

Mild-tasting and a good source of vitamin C and potassium, potatoes make a great first food. Peel and chop, then put into a pan, cover with boiling water, and cook for 15 minutes, or until tender. Alternatively, steam until tender. Use a mouli or sieve to purée, as an electric blender breaks down the starches and produces a sticky pulp. You can also bake potato in an oven for 1–1¼ hours, scoop out the flesh and mash with a little of your baby's usual milk.

Sweet potato

Packed with beta-carotene, sweet potato (see page 60) is a good alternative to ordinary potatoes and it is richer in nutrients. What's more, almost any vegetable when combined with sweet potato will taste delicious. Roasted sweet potato wedges also make a great finger food.

Butternut squash

Another colourful vegetable rich in beta-carotene, butternut squash (see page 63) has a smooth, mild flavour. Try combining it with apple and pear, or keep it simple and just mix with a little baby rice.

Best First Foods

potato

butternut squash

sweet potato

Pumpkin

The orange flesh of this vegetable is sweet and bursting with vitamin C and beta-carotene. Peel and chop, then boil or steam, or bake wedges in the oven (see page 59). Pumpkin purées to a smooth consistency and combines well with fruit, other vegetables, and baby rice, making it a popular early weaning food.

Apple

Apples (see page 64) make an excellent first food for babies that can be puréed to a very smooth consistency. They are a great source of pectin, a soluble fibre that helps your baby's body to process solid food more efficiently.

Pear

Pears (see page 64) also contain pectin and have a sweet, gentle taste that babies love. They are rich in vitamin C and vitamin A, and even contain some B vitamins. Pears need to be cooked only lightly before puréeing, to preserve their nutrient content. If the purée is too runny, stir in a little baby rice to thicken it up.

Banana

Sweet, ripe bananas (see page 66) are the perfect convenience food as they can be prepared without cooking, are a perfect finger food, and can also be simply mashed into a soft purée. Add a little baby milk if the purée is too thick. Bananas contain vitamin C and the mineral potassium, which is needed for a baby's muscle function.

What's more, bananas are little packets of energy, providing three healthy natural sugars. Better still, no other fruit contains more digestible carbohydrates than banana.

WHICH CONSISTENCY?

Your baby's "starter" purées should be semi-liquid – almost the same consistency as yogurt. To begin with she'll seem to suck the food off the spoon. The more liquid the purées are at the outset, the easier your baby will find them to eat.

pumpkin

pear

apple

Papaya

Papaya (see page 66) is another fruit that can be puréed without cooking. Its brightly coloured flesh is rich in essential vitamin C and beta-carotene, and it also contains plenty of fibre, folic acid, and vitamin E, making it a nutritious first food. Most babies love the flavour, too. Papaya contains a natural chemical called "papain", which helps to encourage healthy digestion, and other key nutrients that encourage healthy eyesight.

Mango

Mangoes are rich in vitamins A, B, and C, and contain more calcium than almost any other fruit. They contain a little iron, too. Make sure the mango is ripe, sweet, and not stringy. To prepare the mango, cut it in half either side of the stone, peel away the skin, cut the flesh into cubes, and purée using a hand-blender. Mangoes taste delicious blended with apple, pear, or just about any other fruit to create a wonderful tropical treat for your baby (see page 67).

Sweet, ripe bananas are the perfect convenience food as they can be prepared without cooking, are a perfect finger food, and can also be simply mashed into a soft purée.

Avocado

Avocado (see page 66) is rich in healthy mono-unsaturated fats, which provide energy that encourages your baby's growth and development. It also contributes nearly 20 vitamins, minerals, and beneficial plant compounds to her diet.

It's a perfect, nutrient-dense first food and its smooth consistency makes it ideal for babies. There's no need for cooking, just mash it on its own, or blend with your baby's favourite fruit or vegetable purée. Slices of avocado also make good first finger foods for independent babies.

Best First Foods

banana

mango

papaya

COMBINED PURÉES

Below are some suggestions for flavours that work well together. Start with the main ingredient and then add one, two, or three ingredients as shown. Experiment to find out what your baby likes best.

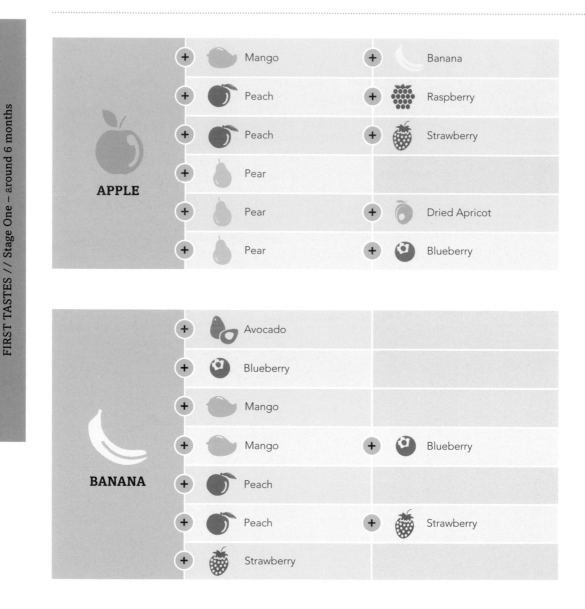

APPLE

+ Mango	+ Banana
+ Peach	+ Raspberry
+ Peach	+ Strawberry
+ Pear	
+ Pear	+ Dried Apricot
+ Pear	+ Blueberry

BANANA

+ Avocado	
+ Blueberry	
+ Mango	
+ Mango	+ Blueberry
+ Peach	
+ Peach	+ Strawberry
+ Strawberry	

Combine for varied flavours and colours.

Make a note of your baby's favourites.

Combined Purées

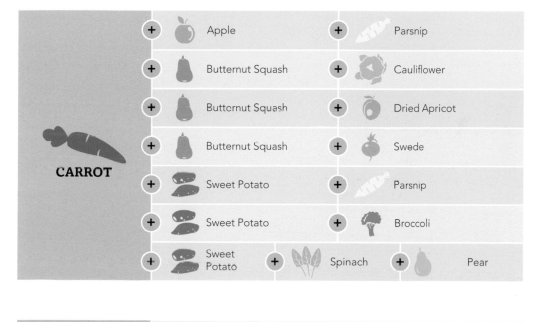

CARROT

+ Apple | + Parsnip
+ Butternut Squash | + Cauliflower
+ Butternut Squash | + Dried Apricot
+ Butternut Squash | + Swede
+ Sweet Potato | + Parsnip
+ Sweet Potato | + Broccoli
+ Sweet Potato + Spinach + Pear

SWEET POTATO

+ Butternut Squash | + Peas
+ Butternut Squash | + Pear
+ Butternut Squash + Carrot + Swede
+ Carrot | + Dried Apricot
+ Parsnip | + Spinach
+ Potato + Peas + Leek

PREPARING YOUR BABY'S MEALS

Providing your baby with healthy, nutritious meals is much easier than you may think when you first start out. Bearing in mind a few basic tips will make sure that he gets the most from the healthy food on offer.

Healthy cooking

Your baby won't be eating much to begin with, so it's important that his food is as nutritious as it can be. Choose produce that is fresh and make sure that your cooking method preserves the nutrients.

Steaming: This is a great way to preserve taste and nutrients, in particular vitamins B and C. You can place the food in a steam basket, sieve, or colander over boiling water and steam until tender. Or, you can steam in the microwave.

> *Your baby won't be eating much at the outset of the weaning process, so it's important that his food is as nutritious as it can be.*

Microwaves: Studies have shown that steaming food in the microwave is safe and leaves nutrients relatively intact. It is equally as good as steaming over boiling water and it's also possible to cook small quantities.

Place the fruit or vegetable in a dish (or microwave steamer), cover (leaving a vent for steam), and cook on full power until tender. Use your baby's usual milk to achieve the right consistency.

Boiling: Although this does tend to rob many fruits and vegetables of their nutrient value, some foods simply don't become soft enough for puréeing using steam. Be sure to use only a small amount of water and save the cooking liquid to thin the puréed food to eating consistency.

Baking or roasting: If you are using your oven to cook a family meal, include some vegetables for your baby. Potato, butternut squash, sweet potato, and pumpkin bake to a nice consistency. Prick the vegetables with a fork and bake until tender, then scoop out the contents and purée.

Food hygiene

Keeping your kitchen clean and using different chopping boards and knives for meat and fruit/vegetables is a good way to keep food-borne illnesses at bay. Puréed food spoils more easily than other food, so must be either used immediately once prepared or placed in the refrigerator once cool, where it will stay fresh for two or three days. Purées can be frozen for future use, and will last for several months in the freezer. By the time your baby reaches weaning age, he'll be putting things into his mouth, so there is no need to sterilize spoons or containers, although they should be washed in hot, soapy water or in the dishwasher, at a temperature high enough to kill germs. It is important, however, to continue to sterilize bottles, particularly the teats. Warm milk is a perfect breeding ground for bacteria.

Puréeing your baby's food

Once your fruit and vegetables are cooked until really tender, you can purée them in a liquidizer or food processor, or with a hand-blender. Potato should be puréed in a mouli (see page 39), or pressed through a sieve. First foods need to be semi-liquid and similar to yogurt in consistency. Add a little of your baby's usual milk in preference to the cooking liquid from the pan or steamer so that you don't dilute the nutrient value.

Batch cooking

This involves cooking larger quantities that can be divided into portions in small pots or ice-cube trays, then frozen in batches. Get into the habit of adding extra portions of fruit and vegetables to the pot when you cook family meals. Bake an extra potato or two, or steam extra broccoli florets, for example. These can be puréed or mashed and then frozen. You can make up combinations by freezing two individual flavours, such as apple and pear, and then defrosting them and mixing them together.

Freezing and reheating

Freezing batches of baby food means you always have something fresh and nutritious on hand to feed your baby. Once you've cooked fruit and vegetables until tender, purée them and then cover. Allow to cool before freezing. Fill the ice-cube trays or pots almost to the top with the purée and store in a freezer that will freeze at −18°C or below within 24 hours. To thaw, take the food out of the freezer several hours before a meal and then reheat until piping hot. Allow to cool before serving. It's important to cook food thoroughly. If you use a microwave, stir carefully and watch out for "hot spots". Do not refreeze meals that have previously been frozen and defrosted. The exception to this is raw frozen food, such as frozen peas, which can be cooked and then re-frozen.

KATE ASKS . . .

I find it easier to buy pouches of organic purées, as I don't have much time for cooking. Is there any real benefit to making baby food at home?

There is nothing wrong with relying on the occasional squeezy pouch of baby food to get you through a busy time, but using them all the time isn't recommended (see page 79). Also be aware that the nutritional content of baby food is compromised because of the heat treatment necessary to make it safe throughout a long shelf life. They also tend to lack the natural sweetness and flavours of fresh foods, and giving mainly pre-prepared baby foods rather than fresh can make it more difficult for your baby to make the transistion to family meals. Although organic baby food is prepared without the use of artificial ingredients, current legislation governing regular baby foods has made it almost impossible for them to contain any pesticides, so organic is unlikely to be superior in any major way.

Batch cooking, puréeing extra portions from family meals, and swapping trays of purées with friends can help to offer a wide range of homemade baby foods.

YOUR BABY'S FIRST "MEAL"

Your baby's first taste of "real" food is a momentous occasion and you'll want to set the scene and choose just the right moment to make it a success. Don't be surprised if things don't go according to plan. Some babies eagerly embrace those first mouthfuls, while others are a little shocked.

Type of weaning

There are three ways of weaning your baby: spoon-feeding, baby-led weaning, and the combined approach (see page 34). In baby-led weaning, you let your baby feed herself. Instead of giving her purées, you offer a range of soft finger foods (see pages 82–83) and cooked soft, but not mushy, vegetables.

Where?

It's a good idea to choose a spot where you'll be regularly feeding your baby, so that she begins to associate it with mealtimes. The kitchen is probably best, as she's bound to make a considerable mess for the first few months – or even years!

In what?

One of the signs of being ready for weaning is being able to sit upright, with or without support. This makes a high chair ideal. As your baby becomes accomplished, you can place food on the tray for her. You may want to use a splash mat to catch any spillages. If you choose to wean before six months and your baby cannot sit upright, use her bouncy chair or car seat to ensure her whole body is supported.

When?

About an hour after your baby's normal milk feed, and after she's had her nap, is a good time to start her on her first tastes in the weaning process. She won't be irritable with hunger, but she may feel a little peckish. Somewhere around midday is ideal. She'll most likely be alert and happy and ready for a new experience. If she's unwell or out of sorts, leave it for another day.

Who should feed your baby?

If you are doing baby-led weaning, your baby will feed herself, with close supervision from you. If you're giving purées, the first spoonfuls are a bit of a momentous event, so mum and dad may want to be on hand to witness her foray into the world of food. However, anyone can successfully feed a young baby, as long as they are patient and allow her to go at her own pace. Some babies respond better to having dad offer the first spoonfuls. If your baby can smell mum's milk, she might resist her new menu in favour of the comfort of something familiar. Similarly, bottle-fed babies may be upset that they are not being offered their usual, warm treat with mum.

Which food?

Baby-led weaning gives babies the opportunity to explore a variety of tastes and textures from the beginning and learn to pick food up and bring it to their mouth. At this first stage, offer a range of finger foods. Eventually, once her hand-to-eye co-ordination is sufficiently developed, your baby will be able to feed herself with a spoon.

The first feed

1 When your baby is happy and settled in her high chair, scoop up a little bit of purée on the end of her spoon and gently hold it to her lips.

2 If your baby opens her mouth, slide the spoon into it and hold it there for a few moments, so she becomes accustomed to the new taste.

3 Carefully withdraw the spoon, using her lips and gums to remove the purée. She may suck at the spoon or even bite down on it with her gums.

4 Refill her spoon and offer a little more. Don't be surprised if most of the purée re-emerges! Simply scoop it back up and try again.

If you're weaning from around six months, a combined fruit or vegetable purée (see pages 46–47) mixed with a little of your baby's usual milk is perfect.

If you are breastfeeding, use a little expressed milk; if you are bottlefeeding, formula is fine. She will be used to the sweet taste of milk and may be put off by the sight and taste of anything new.

Choosing sweet vegetables, or a little baby rice with milk, makes the experience less overwhelming. It's fine to start with single-fruit purées – there's no evidence that this hinders acceptance of vegetables (see page 42).

What consistency?

Adding a little of your baby's usual milk to the purée will make it seem more "familiar" as well as making sure that it is smooth and yogurt-like. To begin with, your baby will "suck" the food from the spoon rather than use her lips to remove it. Until she masters the art

Ready to go. Prepare your baby's first purées so that they have a smooth, yogurt-like consistency, then begin by offering just a few teaspoons per "meal", being careful not to overload the spoon.

of moving the food around her mouth with her tongue, it will need to be liquid enough for her to swallow straight down.

How much?

First foods are simply tastes and textures and her usual milk will remain her major source of nutrition. One or two tablespoons of purée or finger foods once a day is about right for the first week or so, but she may want more or less.

What temperature?

Heat your baby's purée in the microwave or in a small saucepan on the hob. Stir it carefully to make sure that it is evenly heated through, particularly if you are using the microwave, which can create "hot spots". Body temperature is just about right. Test a little on the inside of your wrist, just as you would with formula, and if you can't feel it, that means it is the perfect temperature. If it's too hot, set it to one side for a few minutes.

Which spoon?

Choose a narrow-headed, shallow spoon that fits easily into your baby's mouth. She may not open her mouth for those first few tastes, so your spoon will need to be small enough to slip in. A soft plastic, silicone, or rubber-tipped spoon, known as a "weaning spoon", and suitable from four months onwards, will be friendlier than a cold metal one. Choose a spoon with a shallow "bowl", so that she can easily suck off the contents. You can also give her a chunky plastic spoon to encourage her to feed herself, though she may not be able to do this properly for a while.

Which bowl?

Choose a pot or bowl that you can grip easily, as your baby may reach out and try to grab it. A small bowl makes it easier to scoop up the contents and helps to keep them warm. If your baby is very interested in the bowl and spoon, you can try giving her separate ones to play with and explore. This will help to make it a fun and positive experience for your baby.

How long should it take?

Give your baby plenty of time to get used to things in the early days. She may simply not understand what's required of her, and it may take some time for her to get to grips with the idea that there is food on the spoon. Equally, however, don't continue if she becomes bored or distressed (allow no more than 30 minutes per mealtime). Mealtimes should be fun and pleasurable, so the minute things become tense it's time to stop.

Going it alone. It's a great idea to give your baby his own spoon so he can try to feed himself – or at least chew on it. This helps development of the gag reflex.

What if she doesn't like it?

Some babies can take several sittings before they get used to the idea of having solids so you may need to persevere. It may not be the purée your baby dislikes – it may simply be the whole experience of weaning. Don't forget it is a whole new skill that needs to be learned.

If your baby expresses dislike for a particular purée, take it away and try it again in a few days. You may have to offer your baby the same purée several times before she begins to think of it as being "familiar".

THE NEXT FEW WEEKS

Once you've fed your baby a few teaspoons of purée, or he's eaten some finger foods if you're doing baby-led weaning, you'll feel more confident about introducing new foods. But take it slowly. First foods are all about becoming familiar with new tastes and textures, and the whole concept of swallowing, so your baby won't be ready for full meals for some time yet.

Introducing new foods

If your baby seemed to like a food, make a note of it and continue to offer it. If he doesn't seem to like something, don't give it up – simply reintroduce it a couple of days later, or blend it with a little of his usual milk and try again.

It is no longer recommended that foods are introduced singly if you are weaning from six months. It is a good idea to combine two or more different foods – there is a wide range of combined purées you can make (see pages 46–47). Baby rice or cereals can be blended with any fruit or vegetable purées.

However, a diet of solely fruit and vegetables won't provide a baby of this age with important critical nutrients (see pages 14–17), so you need to provide a balanced diet when you are weaning from six months. See pages 70–71.

You will want to make sure that he is getting at least a spoonful of fruit and vegetables, a carbohydrate (such as pasta, potato, or baby rice), some protein (in the form of lentils, soya, meat, fish, or dairy produce), and some healthy fats, which are also contained in dairy produce, nut butters, ground seeds, and meat. The quantity doesn't matter as much as the variety.

If you or your partner have a history of allergies or your baby has eczema, asthma, or hay fever (see pages 20–27), seek the advice of your doctor.

Combining breast- or bottle-feeding and solid food

Your baby will rely on his usual milk feeds for many months to come, to give him nutrients and comfort. You may want to offer him "meals" halfway through a feed, or at a time when he usually has a smaller feed. His regular morning, midday, evening, and night feeds should continue as usual.

As he progresses towards regular meals, you can slowly reduce the number of milk feeds, or the length of time or amount you feed him. But play it by ear – if he's hungry, he will need to be fed. Until they are a year old, babies need at least 600ml (1 pint) of milk per day. Remember that formula or breast milk added to purées will count towards his overall milk intake. Cow's milk should not be given as a drink until after the first year, as breast milk or formula is a better source of iron and other nutrients. However, it can be used in cooking or with cereal from six months.

Portion sizes

Don't worry too much about the amount of solid food your baby takes in. As long as he is regularly introduced to a variety of fresh, nutritious new foods, you can consider the beginning of the weaning process to be a success. You may also find that your little one is hungrier some days and eats whatever is offered, while on other days he shows little interest at all. Try to go at his pace and let his interest levels and hunger dictate how much he is fed.

Cooking in advance. Preparing batches of purées and freezing them helps make sure that you always have baby food to hand.

The Next Few Weeks

YOUR BABY'S RESPONSE

When a beautifully prepared purée is met with resistance, you may feel that all your careful preparation has gone to waste. There are, however, solutions to almost any problem that crops up. If you're doing baby-led weaning, it may feel as if your baby is eating very little to begin with. The important thing is to avoid panicking and go at your baby's pace.

My baby always wants more

Many parents would consider this to be a good thing, but if you are concerned that your baby is eating more than she should, or putting on excess weight, then you may want to contact your Health Visitor or GP. Most babies won't want more than the equivalent of a few tablespoons of purée at the outset, although some are hungrier than others. Make sure your baby is getting enough of her usual milk – she may genuinely need more milk for her growth and development.

My baby refuses to open her mouth

First of all, check that you aren't anxious when you are feeding her. If she senses that her clamped lips are getting a response from you she may well continue – and even consider it a game. Try to use distraction. Get her to look up at something on the ceiling, causing her mouth to fall open. Slip in a little food and

Meeting milk needs. Make sure your baby is getting enough of her usual milk (600ml/1 pint) alongside her first purées.

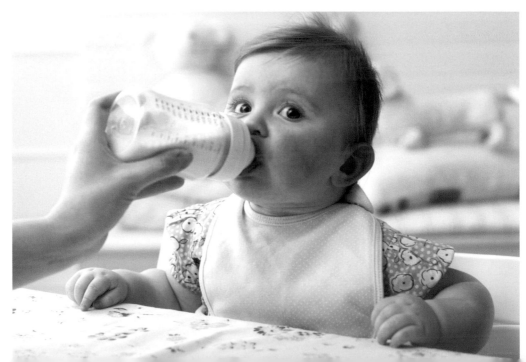

see how she gets on. If she resists the spoon, try either rubbing a little purée on her lips or dip a clean finger in it and allow her to suck it. You can also offer her a little bowl of purée, in which she can dip her fingers (which will eventually end up in her mouth). Try eating a little yourself – many babies are happy to mimic mum or dad!

She cries when I sit her down to eat

It might help to have dad or other familiar person feed her. Breastfed babies, in particular, associate mum with the comfort of breast-feeding – they can smell your milk and may become upset when it isn't on offer. Try sitting her on your lap and holding her closely when you feed her or perhaps sitting her in her high chair to play with toys. You may need to give weaning a miss for a few days, or distraction sometimes helps. If all else fails, place a little purée on her tray and let her experiment herself.

My baby started on solids, but is now refusing them

It's not unusual for babies to regress – it's a big developmental leap to adjust to eating new and different foods, and to give up the comfort of milk feeds. Try to make the process easier by offering your baby plenty of milk after her "meals". Continue to offer new foods daily, but try to stay relaxed and calm if she rejects them. She'll eventually become accustomed to the new routine, and look forward to mealtimes, particularly if they are fun and you praise her.

My baby doesn't like the spoon

Babies are unable to lick food from a spoon with their tongue so make sure you are using a spoon that is soft-tipped and shallow (see page 52). Give her one of her own to hold, too. Try using a piece of toast to scoop up some purée and let her suck that to help her get used to the idea. There is no harm in letting her try to feed herself, using her hands.

She only likes sweet purées

Babies are programmed to like sweet tastes – breast milk is sweet. Try introducing sweet-tasting vegetables, such as sweet potato, and when she is hungrier give a vegetable purée rather than fruit. Combine fruit and vegetables, then gradually reduce the amount of fruit.

My baby misses the closeness of breastfeeding

Many babies find the transition to solids difficult and it's not surprising that a spoon with mysterious contents doesn't hold much allure. Try sitting your baby on your lap and holding her close. To begin, it can help to feed her a little expressed milk on a spoon, to help her adjust. From there, gradually add a little baby rice, or fruit and vegetable purées.

I'm trying baby-led weaning, but without much success so far

Not all babies have sufficient hand-to-eye co-ordination for baby-led weaning. It might be better to start with spoon-feeding before moving on to soft finger foods. There is nothing wrong with a combined approach (see page 35).

Sweet veggies first. Your baby will be used to the sweet taste of milk, so it's a good idea to start the weaning process with sweet vegetable purées such as carrot.

Carrots are a perfect starter food for your baby, with plenty of nutrients and a sweet taste and smooth texture. You can prepare other root vegetables, such as sweet potato, swede, and parsnip, using this method, too.

FIRST VEGETABLES

⬡ **Suitable for freezing**
Makes 4 portions • Suitable from 20 weeks • Prep time 5 minutes • Cooking time 15–20 minutes • Provides vitamin A, vitamin C, fibre

2 medium carrots, peeled, chopped or sliced
A little breast milk or formula (optional)

1 Put the carrots in a steamer set over boiling water. Cover and steam for 15–20 minutes, until the carrots are really tender.

2 Purée the carrots until smooth in a food processor or place in a bowl and use a hand-blender, adding a little water from the steamer or some of your baby's usual milk to get the right consistency. First purées should be quite runny.

3 Freeze in individual portions. When needed, thaw overnight in the fridge or for 1–2 hours at room temperature, then microwave or reheat in a small pan until piping hot. Stir and allow to cool before serving.

Variation: Place the carrots in a saucepan, cover with boiling water, then bring back to the boil. Reduce the heat, cover, and simmer for about 15 minutes before puréeing, as above.

For baby-led weaning, cut a carrot into sticks 6cm (2¹/₂in) long and 1cm (¹/₂in) wide. Steam until fairly soft. Leave to cool before serving.

Roasting root vegetables brings out their natural sugars and flavour. Both butternut squash and pumpkin make good first weaning foods, as they are easily digested and unlikely to cause an allergic reaction. Pop some in the oven when you are cooking a meal for the family, and then whizz until smooth.

ROASTED BUTTERNUT SQUASH OR PUMPKIN

❄ **Suitable for freezing**
Makes 6–8 portions • Suitable from 20 weeks • Prep time 5 minutes • Cooking time 45 minutes • Provides vitamin A, vitamin C, fibre

1 small butternut squash or
¹/₂ small pumpkin (about
700g/1¹/₂lb)
A little breast milk or formula
(optional)

1 Preheat the oven to 200°C (fan 180°C), gas 6.

2 Halve the butternut squash. Scoop out the seeds and fibrous strings from both halves. Place the squash or pumpkin cut-side down on a well-oiled baking tray lined with baking paper and bake for about 45 minutes, or until the squash is tender.

3 Remove from the oven and allow to cool. Scoop out the flesh and purée until smooth using a stick blender. Add a little of your baby's usual milk to thin the consistency if your baby prefers.

4 Freeze in individual portions. When needed, thaw overnight in the fridge or for 1–2 hours at room temperature, then microwave or reheat in a small pan until piping hot. Stir and allow to cool before serving.

Variation: Steam the butternut squash or pumpkin. Cut in half and scrape out the seeds and fibrous strings and discard. Peel and cut into cubes. Place in a steamer and steam for 12–15 minutes, or until tender. Purée until smooth as above.

For baby-led weaning, cut the butternut squash or pumpkin into batons about 6cm (2¹/₂in) long and 1cm (¹/₂in) wide and steam for 10–12 minutes, or until tender.

Sweet potato is a great source of beta-carotene (this is converted into vitamin A in your baby's body), and a variety of other nutrients. Unlike ordinary potato, it can be easily mashed or puréed without becoming too starchy. It also freezes well.

BAKED SWEET POTATO

❄ **Suitable for freezing**

Makes 6 portions • Suitable from 20 weeks • Prep time 3 minutes • Cooking time 1 hour • Provides vitamin A, vitamin C, fibre

2 small sweet potatoes (about 500g/1lb 2oz, in total)

A little breast milk or formula (optional)

1 Preheat the oven to 200°C (fan 180°C), gas 6.

2 Scrub the potatoes and prick with a metal skewer or fork. Place on a baking sheet and bake for about 1 hour, or until wrinkled and tender.

3 Remove from the oven, cut the potatoes in half, scoop out the flesh, and purée in a food processor or place in a bowl and use a hand-blender. You can add a little of your baby's usual milk to thin the consistency if your baby prefers.

4 Freeze in individual portions. When needed, thaw overnight in the fridge or for 1–2 hours at room temperature, then microwave or reheat in a small pan until piping hot. Stir and allow to cool before serving.

Variation: Combine baked sweet potato with baked butternut squash for a highly nutritious purée. Lay a large piece of foil on a baking sheet and spread cubes of squash and sweet potato on the foil. For babies under six months, you can brush the sweet potato and butternut squash with a little sunflower oil. For babies aged six months old and over, cut a knob of unsalted butter into pieces and dot over, then sprinkle with water. Cover with a second large piece of foil and scrunch the edges of the two foil pieces together to form a parcel. Bake for about 30 minutes, or until the vegetables are tender. Cool the vegetables slightly then purée in a food processor (including any liquid). You can thin the purée with a little breast milk or formula if your baby prefers.

For baby-led weaning, scrub the sweet potato but don't peel it. Cut into wedges and arrange on a baking tray. Brush with a little oil and roast for 20–25 minutes at 180°C (fan 160°C), gas 4.

Any root vegetable will work beautifully in this recipe. They purée to a smooth consistency, and have a mild flavour that babies love.

TRIO OF ROOT VEGETABLES

❄ **Suitable for freezing**

Makes 5 portions • Suitable from 20 weeks • Prep time 10 minutes • Cooking time 20 minutes • Provides vitamin A, vitamin C, fibre

1 large carrot, peeled and diced

1 small sweet potato (about 250g/9oz), peeled and diced

1 small parsnip, peeled and diced

A little breast milk or formula (optional)

1 Put the vegetables in a steamer set over boiling water. Cover and steam for 20 minutes until soft.

2 Purée until smooth in a food processor or place in a bowl and use a hand-blender, adding a little water from the steamer or some of your baby's usual milk, if needed, to get the right consistency.

3 Freeze in individual portions. Thaw overnight in the fridge or for 1–2 hours at room temperature, then microwave or reheat in a small pan until piping hot. Stir and allow to cool before serving.

Variation: You can boil the vegetables for 18–20 minutes, until tender, before puréeing, but you will lose some of the nutrients. Vitamins B and C are water-soluble, so the best way to preserve them is by steaming or baking.

Trio of Root Vegetables

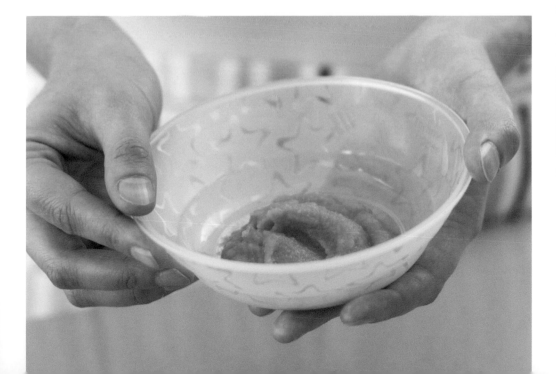

Combining vegetables with fruit is a great way to tempt your baby. All babies seem to love sweet tastes, and breastfed babies, who are used to the naturally sweet flavour of breast milk, will be enchanted!

CARROT, SWEET POTATO, AND APPLE

❄ **Suitable for freezing**

Makes 4 portions • Suitable from 20 weeks • Prep time 8 minutes • Cooking time 14 minutes • Provides vitamin A, vitamin C, fibre

1 medium carrot, peeled and sliced

1 small sweet potato (about 250g/9oz), peeled and diced

1 sweet eating apple (eg Pink Lady or Gala), peeled, cored, and cut into small chunks

A little breast milk or formula (optional)

1 Steam the carrot and sweet potato for 8 minutes. Add the apple and steam for another 6 minutes.

2 Purée in a food processor or place in a bowl and use a hand-blender. Thin to the desired consistency with a little water from the bottom of the steamer or a little of your baby's usual milk.

3 Freeze in individual portions. When needed, thaw overnight in the fridge or for 1–2 hours at room temperature, then microwave or reheat in a small pan until piping hot. Stir and allow to cool before serving.

For baby-led weaning, serve peeled apple wedges and steamed sticks of carrot and sweet potato.

The sweet flavour of butternut squash blends beautifully with the fruitiness of apple to make this the perfect purée for even the fussiest baby.

BUTTERNUT SQUASH AND APPLE

❄ **Suitable for freezing**

Makes 4 portions • Suitable from 20 weeks • Prep time 10 minutes • Cooking time 12 minutes
• Provides vitamin A, vitamin C, fibre • Dairy-free

½ small butternut squash, peeled and diced (about 350g/12oz)

1 sweet eating apple (eg Pink Lady or Gala), peeled, cored, and cut into chunks

1 Steam the butternut squash for 6 minutes. Add the apple chunks and steam for a further 6 minutes, or until both are tender.

2 Purée the squash and apple in a food processor or place in a bowl and use a hand-blender, adding 2 tablespoons of liquid from the steamer.

3 Freeze in individual portions. When needed, thaw overnight in the fridge or for 1–2 hours at room temperature, then microwave or reheat in a small pan until piping hot. Stir and allow to cool before serving.

For baby-led weaning, serve peeled apple wedges and steamed squash.

The gentle sweetness of pears works well with any vegetable purée. Bursting with nutrients, this is an ideal first combination for your little one.

BUTTERNUT SQUASH AND PEAR

❄ **Suitable for freezing**

Makes 4 portions • Suitable from 20 weeks • Prep time 10 minutes • Cooking time 12 minutes
• Provides vitamin A, vitamin C, fibre • Dairy-free

½ small butternut squash, peeled and diced (about 350g/12oz)

1 medium-sized ripe pear, peeled and cut into chunks

1 Steam the butternut squash for 8 minutes. Add the pear and steam for a further 2–4 minutes, depending on how ripe the pear is.

2 Purée in a food processor or place in a bowl and use a hand-blender. You probably won't need to add any liquid, but if you think the purée is too thick add a tablespoon or two of the liquid from the steamer.

3 Freeze in individual portions. Thaw overnight in the fridge or for 1–2 hours at room temperature, then microwave or reheat in a small pan until piping hot. Stir and allow to cool before serving.

For baby-led weaning, serve peeled pear wedges and steamed squash.

Apples are ideal first fruits for weaning as they are easy to digest and unlikely to cause allergies. For extra flavour, simmer the apples with a small cinnamon stick, and discard before puréeing.

APPLE PURÉE

❄ **Suitable for freezing**

Makes 4 portions • Suitable from 20 weeks • Prep time 5 minutes
• Cooking time 6–8 minutes • Provides vitamin C, fibre

2 sweet eating apples (eg Pink Lady, Gala, or Jazz), peeled, cored, and diced
60–75ml (4–5 tbsp) water

1 Put the diced apple into a heavy-based saucepan with the water. Cover and cook over a low heat for 6–8 minutes, until really tender.

2 Purée in a food processor or place in a bowl and use a hand-blender, or beat with a wooden spoon, until smooth. Freeze in individual portions, and thaw as described for pear below.

Variation: You can also steam the apples for 7–8 minutes until tender, then purée. Add some of the water from the bottom of the steamer or some pure apple juice to thin the purée if your baby prefers.

For baby-led weaning, peel and core the apple and cut into wedges.

Pears are deliciously sweet and can be easily prepared for even the smallest babies. If the purée is too runny, stir in a little baby rice to help thicken it.

PEAR PURÉE

❄ **Suitable for freezing**

Makes 4 portions • Suitable from 20 weeks • Prep time 2 minutes
• Cooking time 4–6 minutes • Provides vitamin C, fibre

2 large or 4 small ripe pears, cored and cut into quarters

1 Put the pears in a steamer, cover, and steam for 4–6 minutes depending on ripeness. Remove, allow to cool, then peel away the skin.

2 Purée in a food processor or place in a bowl and use a hand-blender, or mash with a fork, until smooth.

3 Freeze in individual portions. When needed, thaw overnight in the fridge or for 1–2 hours at room temperature before serving.

For baby-led weaning, peel a ripe pear and cut into wedges.

Planning ahead.
Making a larger quantity of apple purée then freezing several portions in an ice-cube tray helps save on time spent cooking.

There are many purées that don't need any cooking at all. All these fruits are very nutritious and can be prepared in minutes. They each make one portion and are best eaten fresh, although you can freeze papaya if you like.

NO COOK PURÉES

Banana

Suitable from 20 weeks • Provides potassium, B vitamins, fibre

½ small, ripe banana
A little breast milk or formula (optional)

Simply mash the banana with a fork until smooth. If the purée is too thick for your baby, you can thin it with a little of your baby's usual milk.

Papaya

Suitable from 20 weeks • Provides vitamin A, vitamin C, fibre

½ small, ripe papaya

Cut a small papaya in half and remove the black seeds. Scoop the flesh into a bowl and mash with a fork until smooth.

Avocado

Suitable from 20 weeks • Provides energy, B vitamins, monounsaturated fatty acids, fibre, vitamin E

½ small, ripe avocado
A little breast milk or formula

Cut the avocado in half and remove the stone. Scoop out the flesh into a bowl and mash together with a little of your baby's usual milk.

Variation: A popular purée combination that is very nutritious is mashed avocado and banana. Place the sliced banana and the avocado flesh into a bowl and mash together.

Peach and Banana

Suitable from 20 weeks • Provides vitamin C, fibre

1 large, ripe peach
1 small, ripe banana, sliced
A little baby rice or full-fat plain yogurt
   or dairy-free alternative

Peel the peach (see tip, page 95) and then cut the flesh from the stone and mash together with the sliced banana using a fork or, if preferred, use a hand-blender. (If you like, you can put the peach and banana into a small saucepan and cook for a minute or two before puréeing.) Serve this purée on its own or mixed with a little baby rice or yogurt.

For baby-led weaning, cut a banana into 5–6cm (2–2½in) chunks and give to your baby as a finger food, along with unpeeled slices of peach.

When sweet ripe mangoes are in season they make wonderful baby food as they don't need any cooking. They are also rich in beta-carotene and vitamin C. Each recipe makes two portions and takes minutes to prepare. All are suitable for freezing apart from Mango and Banana.

MANGO PURÉES

Mango Purée

Suitable from 20 weeks • Provides vitamin C, fibre

½ medium-sized, ripe mango
A little breast milk or formula (optional)

Remove the skin from the mango half, cut all the flesh off the stone and you should have about 115g (4oz) flesh. Purée in a food processor or put in a bowl and use a hand-blender or mash thoroughly with a fork until smooth. Add some of your baby's usual milk, if needed, to reach the desired consistency.

Mango and Banana

Suitable from 20 weeks • Provides fibre, vitamin C, potassium

½ small, ripe mango
½ small banana

Prepare the mango as for Mango Purée (see left). Slice the banana. Purée together in a food processor or put in a bowl and use a hand-blender or mash thoroughly together with a fork until smooth.

Creamy Mango

Suitable from 20 weeks • Provides calcium, vitamin C, fibre, protein

½ small, ripe mango
2 tbsp full-fat plain yogurt or dairy-free alternative

Prepare the mango as for Mango Purée (see above). Put in a bowl and purée with a hand-blender or mash thoroughly with a fork until smooth, then beat in the yogurt.

For baby-led weaning, peel a ripe mango and cut into wedges.

Mango and Apple

Suitable from 20 weeks • Provides vitamin C, fibre

½ small, ripe mango
2 tbsp apple purée (see page 64)

Prepare the mango as for Mango Purée (see above left) and place in a bowl. Purée the mango flesh together with the apple purée using a hand-blender or simply mash the mango thoroughly with a fork and beat in the apple purée.

Mango Purées

The planners on these pages introduce solids to babies who are weaned early (see page 30). Note: a baby must never be weaned before 17 weeks. A young baby will journey through weaning at a slower, gentler pace than an older baby.

BEFORE 6 MONTHS: FIRST TASTES

MENU PLANNER 1					
DAY	**EARLY MORNING**	**BREAKFAST**	**LUNCH**	**TEA**	**BEDTIME**
1	Breast/bottle	Breast/bottle	Carrot purée (p.58) or Baked Sweet Potato (p.60) Breast/bottle	Breast/bottle	Breast/bottle
2	Breast/bottle	Breast/bottle	Roasted Butternut Squash (p.59) Breast/bottle	Breast/bottle	Breast/bottle
3	Breast/bottle	Breast/bottle	Apple Purée (p.64) Breast/bottle	Breast/bottle	Breast/bottle
4	Breast/bottle	Breast/bottle	Potato purée or Swede purée Breast/bottle	Breast/bottle	Breast/bottle
5	Breast/bottle	Breast/bottle	Pear Purée (p.64) with baby rice Breast/bottle	Breast/bottle	Breast/bottle
6	Breast/bottle	Breast/bottle	Carrot purée (p.58) or Baked Sweet Potato (p.60) Breast/bottle	Breast/bottle	Breast/bottle
7	Breast/bottle	Breast/bottle	Roasted Butternut Squash (p.59) Breast/bottle	Breast/bottle	Breast/bottle

Let your baby be the guide as to when he moves to two meals a day. Repeat meals on consecutive days if you wish. In addition to the milk feeds shown, your baby may also need one mid-morning, mid-afternoon, and during the night.

WHEN YOUR BABY IS READY FOR MORE

MENU PLANNER 2					
DAY	**EARLY MORNING**	**BREAKFAST**	**LUNCH**	**TEA**	**BEDTIME**
1	Breast/bottle	Apple Purée (p.64) Breast/bottle	Baked Sweet Potato (p.60) or Roasted Squash (p.59)/Breast/bottle	Breast/bottle	Breast/bottle
2	Breast/bottle	Banana Purée (p.66) Breast/bottle	Trio of Root Vegetables (p.61) Breast/bottle	Breast/bottle	Breast/bottle
3	Breast/bottle	Mango and Banana Purée (p.67) Breast/bottle	Sweet Potato and broccoli Breast/bottle	Breast/bottle	Breast/bottle
4	Breast/bottle	Apple and Pear Purée (p.64) with baby cereal Breast/bottle	Carrot Purée (p.58) Breast/bottle	Breast/bottle	Breast/bottle
5	Breast/bottle	Banana Purée (p.66) or Papaya Purée (p.66) Breast/bottle	Trio of Root Vegetables (p.61) Breast/bottle	Breast/bottle	Breast/bottle
6	Breast/bottle	Apple Purée (p.64) with baby cereal Breast/bottle	Sweet Potato and broccoli Breast/bottle	Breast/bottle	Breast/bottle
7	Breast/bottle	Peach and Banana Purée (p.66) Breast/bottle	Butternut Squash and Apple (p.63) Breast/bottle	Breast/bottle	Breast/bottle

When weaning from six months, you should progress onto highly nutritious foods more quickly to get critical nutrients on board. In addition to the milk feeds shown, your baby may also need a mid-afternoon and night-time feed.

MENU PLANNER: FROM AROUND 6 MONTHS

WEEK 1					
DAY	EARLY MORNING	BREAKFAST	LUNCH	TEA	BEDTIME
1	Breast/bottle	Breast/bottle	Puréed vegetables	Breast/bottle	Breast/bottle
2	Breast/bottle	Breast/bottle	Puréed fruit	Breast/bottle	Breast/bottle
3	Breast/bottle	Breast/bottle	Avocado, sliced lengthways	Breast/bottle	Breast/bottle
4	Breast/bottle	Breast/bottle	Sticks of steamed carrot	Breast/bottle	Breast/bottle
5	Breast/bottle	Breast/bottle	Whole Greek natural yogurt	Breast/bottle	Breast/bottle
6	Breast/bottle	Breast/bottle	Lentil Purée with Sweet Potato (p.95)	Breast/bottle	Breast/bottle
7	Breast/bottle	Breast/bottle	Apple Purée and Pear Purée (p.64)	Breast/bottle	Breast/bottle

WEEK 2

DAY	EARLY MORNING	BREAKFAST	LUNCH	TEA	BEDTIME
1	Breast/bottle	Purple Porridge (p.86)	Lentil Purée with Sweet Potato (p.95) Sliced nectarines	Breast/bottle	Breast/bottle
2	Breast/bottle	Finger of wholemeal toast with butter	Scrambled egg Sliced kiwi	Breast/bottle	Breast/bottle
3	Breast/bottle	Sliced strawberries	Penne pasta with a little melted butter and grated cheese Whole Greek natural yogurt swirled with a nut butter or fruit purée	Breast/bottle	Breast/bottle
4	Breast/bottle	Iron-fortified breakfast cereal e.g. Weetabix	Poached Salmon with Carrots and Peas (p.99) or flaked salmon with steamed carrot sticks Yogurt and fruit purée	Breast/bottle	Breast/bottle
5	Breast/bottle	Finger of toast with cream cheese	Beef Casserole with Sweet Potato (p.116) Banana	Breast/bottle	Breast/bottle
6	Breast/bottle	Iron-fortified cereal e.g. Rice Krispies	Chicken and Parsnip Purée (p.110) Sliced pear	Breast/bottle	Breast/bottle
7	Breast/bottle	Finger of toast with thin spread of peanut butter	Sliced boiled egg Avocado, sliced lengthways Whole Greek yogurt and fruit purée	Breast/bottle	Breast/bottle

Meal Planner: from around 6 Months

Exploring new tastes and textures

Stage Two – 6 to 9 months

By now, your baby should **have a good repertoire** of foods providing all the critical nutrients she needs to **maximize her development.** Her diet should include dairy produce, meat, poultry, and fish, as well as an **increasing variety** of fruits and vegetables. Experimenting with new tastes and textures is a very important part of **successful weaning.**

• *Menu planner page 121*

THE BEST NEW FOODS

Once first tastes have been established, adding variety to your baby's diet is essential. Choosing from a wide range of nutritious foods will make preparing meals even more enjoyable. You can begin to get to work on creating truly balanced meals for your baby.

Grains and cereals

All cereal grains can be offered from the start of weaning, as long as your baby can manage the texture. There is no need to avoid gluten as previously advised. Breakfast cereals are a good weaning food as most branded cereals are fortified with iron. You don't have to buy special baby cereals which are, in fact, often unfortified and so not as nutritious. Porridge oats and millet contain a natural source of iron and protein. Ready Brek and Weetabix have additional iron added, but some instant oats don't, so check the food label. Don't give sugar-coated or chocolate cereals as they are exceptionally unhealthy and are unsuitable for babies. Also avoid bran cereals as they contain insoluble fibre (see page 16).

Give a mixture of white and wholemeal bread, pasta, and rice to ensure your baby doesn't get too much fibre. White bread is fortified with nutrients, but wholemeal bread has an easier texture for a baby to manage.

Eggs

As a lifelong fan of dippy eggs with soldiers, it was fantastic to hear that the government has issued new advice confirming that runny eggs are safe for everyone to eat, as long as you make sure you look for the British Lion mark. Replacing the previous warning that vulnerable groups such as pregnant women, babies, and young children should eat only fully cooked eggs, the guidance follows a year-long risk assessment by the Food Standards Agency. Eggs are incredibly nutritious, packed full of protein, iron, omega-3 fatty acids, selenium, folate, vitamin D, and lots more good stuff. There is emerging evidence to suggest that introducing eggs when weaning may reduce the risk of egg allergy later in childhood.

Red meat

Iron deficiency is the commonest nutritional deficiency in young children. In the UK, one in five babies between six months and two years has below the desired level. Red meat provides the best source of iron as well as

Nutritious eggs. Eggs are ideal for weaning – give them as part of a meal or as a healthy snack.

What's on the menu today?

Get the balance right for your baby.

protein and other nutrients. Babies often reject red meat not because of its taste but because of its lumpy texture. Start with cooked lean beef or liver, purée to a smooth consistency, and combine well with fruit. Slowly cook lean stewing steak in a casserole with root vegetables and fruit, and purée to the desired consistency. You can then move on to cooked minced meat, which you can whizz in a blender to make it easier for your baby to swallow.

Chicken

You can combine chicken with root vegetables, such as carrot or sweet potato, to give it a smooth texture, or add fruit such as apple to give it a slightly sweet taste. The brown meat of the chicken contains more iron and zinc than the breast. Chunks of white meat can also be offered as finger food.

Fish

The importance of fish can't be overemphasized and fish should be introduced at six months. The healthy fats (EFAs) contained in oily fish such as salmon encourage growth and are essential for your baby's brain development and important for the development of the nervous system and vision. Babies should have two portions of oily fish a week, but not more due to concerns about pollutants. However, babies can eat an unlimited amount of white fish. Fish is good mixed with vegetables and pieces of cooked fish can be given as finger food.

Dairy products

Babies grow at a rapid rate, so you should give full-fat milk and dairy products. Always choose pasteurized cheeses and avoid blue cheese, Brie, Camembert, and feta until your baby reaches 12 months. Offer fresh yogurt, but watch out for fromage frais and yogurts that contain high levels of sugar and other additives.

> " The importance of fish can't be overemphasized and fish should be introduced at six months "

Fruit and vegetables

Both contain vitamin C, which helps your baby absorb iron, so offer them at every meal. You can purée fruits, add them to cooked dishes, such as combining apple with chicken, or give them as a finger food. Lightly steamed vegetables also make great finger foods.

Pulses

Butter beans, lentils, and other dried peas and beans provide lots of protein, iron, and fibre. Larger beans can be cooked and offered as finger food, and most beans and peas mash up well for purées – push them through a sieve, if necessary, to remove tough skins.

The Best New Foods

FOODS TO AVOID

Although your baby will now be able to eat a wide variety of different foods, there are some that will need to wait until a little bit later. It's important to remember that your baby will not be ready for adult food just yet, and you'll need to take care to avoid rich, fatty, spicy, salty, and sugary foods to make sure he stays healthy.

Fatty foods

Babies need plenty of fat in their diet for growth and development and to keep their energy levels high. It is, however, important to choose healthy fats (see pages 14–16) and to avoid very fatty foods. In particular, deep-fried food is a bad idea for most babies, as are foods cooked in a lot of butter or oil, but it is okay to stir-fry or sauté with olive, rapeseed, or sunflower oil.

Honey

Honey is not recommended for babies under the age of one because there is a small risk of contracting botulism. For this reason, infants under 12 months of age should never be fed honey, even if pasteurized.

Unpasteurized dairy products

Dairy products, such as milk, cheese, and yogurt, must be pasteurized to prevent the risk of bacterial infection. Cow's milk as a main drink is not appropriate for babies under 12 months of age, although it can be used with cereal and in cooking from six months and in other forms such as cheese, butter, and yogurt.

Avoid giving your baby soft cheeses such as Brie, or those with "mould" such as blue cheese. Always choose full-fat dairy products, not low-fat ones, as your baby needs energy (see pages 14–16).

The right cheese. Any cheese you give to your baby must be pasteurized.

Additives and preservatives

Artificial sweeteners, flavours, and other additives and preservatives should be avoided. Processed foods almost always contain artificial nasties, and also tend to be high in unhealthy forms of fat and sugar, so should not be offered to babies. However, if you do choose to buy your baby's food, look out for E numbers, which are the numbers given to additives. E300 to 304 (vitamin C) and E307 to 309 (vitamin E) are okay, but make sure you avoid any others. There should be no added salt or sugar, and most definitely no trans fats – you'll find these listed on the label as "hydrogenated".

Fresh, whole foods are best for your baby.

Keep salt and sugar off the menu.

Salt

Excessive salt can cause long-term damage to your baby – in particular, to his kidneys. A tiny bit used in cooking is acceptable, but generally avoid adding it to food and avoid buying foods that contain it – processed meats are particularly high in salt. If you use stock cubes in purées, dilute them well and opt for low-salt or unsalted brands. As your baby isn't accustomed to salt he won't miss the taste in the way that you might. He'll grow to enjoy the natural sweet and savoury flavours of fresh foods.

Sugar

Babies are born with mature sweet taste buds and so have a natural affinity for sweet foods. If your baby gets used to sugar early on, he'll not only be more likely to develop a sweet tooth but his teeth may also be damaged.

What's more, excess sugar in your baby's diet can lead to obesity in later life. Fruits are naturally sweet and root vegetables have a natural sweetness that babies like. Unless you need to use sugar in the occasional baked treat or to sweeten very tart fruit, I would recommend leaving it off the menu.

Naturally sweet. Fruit contains natural sugars that will satisfy a baby who has a sweet tooth.

AN UPDATE ON NUTS

At one time, nuts would have appeared in this list of foods to avoid. However, guidelines have changed because there is no clear evidence that eating or not eating peanuts during pregnancy, while breastfeeding, or during early infant life influences the chances of a child developing a nut allergy. Very finely ground nuts, and nut butters, are a healthy addition to your baby's diet, and research indicates that early introduction may help to prevent allergies (see page 20), although more research is required. If you have a family history of allergies or eczema, watch your baby carefully. Never give whole nuts to children under five due to the risk of choking.

LUMPS, CHUNKS, AND LEARNING TO CHEW

It's normal to worry that your baby might choke if you offer lumpy foods and finger foods, but it's important for her development to add them to her diet – and as soon as you can after she's six months old.

A sensory experience

Learning to eat is a complex experience, involving how the food looks, smells, tastes, and feels, and even how it sounds as it is being eaten. Eating makes your baby more body conscious as she learns to recognize sensations such as hunger and thirst, and learning to chew helps develop the oral motor muscles that help speech development.

Given all this, it is important to introduce different textures and flavours as early as possible when weaning. Even at the purée stage, home-made purées will introduce different textures; ready-made varieties are often of a uniform consistency.

Some parents regularly feed their baby ready-made food from pouches and recent research in the US highlighted that therapists are seeing a big problem with babies fed this way. The babies are not being exposed to variations in sight, sound, touch, taste, and smell and because they are sucking from the pouch, they also aren't developing the important motor skills that come from learning to chew.

Introducing lumpy food

Learning to chew is important – recent research found that if there is delay in giving foods a baby needs to chew beyond 10 months, the baby is less likely to be eating family meals at two years of age as he hasn't developed the skills at the optimum time. You don't need to

Going lumpy. It's a good idea to start stirring tiny pasta shapes into your baby's purées to encourage her to chew.

wait until your baby's teeth have come through to introduce lumpy food. Her full set of teeth are hidden under her gums. Some babies are slow to adapt to chewing, but giving smooth purées for too long can affect your baby learning to chew.

Accepting lumpy food can still be a problem if you've taken the baby-led weaning route (see page 34) and not given many purées – your baby may happily chew on soft finger foods, but still refuse lumpy food later on. That's because learning to eat lumps is more complicated as your baby has to deal with more than one texture in her mouth.

Babies tend to prefer an overall lumpy texture rather than a purée with the occasional surprise lumps, so introduce lumps gradually. For example, use your baby's favourite purée as a pasta sauce. You can also add mashed, grated, and finely chopped foods to your baby's diet.

Finger foods

Once your baby has mastered soft finger foods, such as buttered toast, banana, and a stick of avocado, and can bite and chew them, you may find that she is ready for foods such as raw carrots and apple. Keep a close eye on your baby when you give her hard food to chew, in case she bites off a large piece that she can't manage. Always stay with your child and watch her closely when she is eating.

Teething

When your baby is teething, she may lose her appetite, have runnier stools, and be unsettled at night. The following may help to soothe discomfort so that she can eat normally:

- Giving a refrigerated dummy or teether.
- Giving chilled fruit, such as banana or peach.
- Chewing on chilled hard foods such as carrot and cucumber – you can hold one end while your baby chews on the other.
- Putting a clean wet flannel in an unused plastic bag and chilling it in the fridge. Your baby will find it soothing to chew on the cloth.
- You can buy teething gels (always choose sugar-free) in the chemist. These usually contain a local anaesthetic. The gel usually washes away with the baby's saliva, so the effects may not last long.

Gagging and choking

All babies will gag during weaning because their mouths are quite sensitive and the gag reflex is close to the front of their mouths. A gagging baby will cough and splutter, her eyes will water and she may become upset. If your

> *Almost all babies will gag during weaning because their mouths are quite sensitive and the gag reflex is close to the front of their mouths.*

baby gags on food, it's important to try to let her deal with it – it's a normal safety reflex that pushes food towards the front of the mouth for further chewing or to spit it out.

To help your baby manage her gag reflex, let her self-feed long stick-shaped foods. Once she knows how to deal with gagging, she will have learned how much chewing different foods need.

Choking, however, is when the airway is blocked – a choking baby is likely to be silent and will require urgent assistance.

If your baby is choking

Lay her face down on your forearm, with her head positioned lower than her chest. With the other hand, give five sharp whacks to her mid-back. Ask someone to call an ambulance. **Note**: I highly recommend attending a baby first-aid course before you start weaning.

To prevent choking

Don't give your baby finger foods if she is on her own or if she is seated in an outward-facing pushchair.

- Avoid giving raw vegetables or chunks of hard cheese until your baby can chew them properly. You can, however, give grated versions of these foods.
- Don't give whole nuts or fruits with stones.
- Offer large pieces of vegetables and fruit that your baby can hold in her fist.
- Cut grapes, cherry tomatoes, and giant blueberries in half.

" Sam and Toby, 8 months

Toby was a good eater when I first started to wean him and he devoured most of the fresh purées I made. I felt pretty confident about including some lumpy bits and began by mashing some of the fruits and vegetables and mixing them with his usual purées. He not only refused these point blank, but spent most of the meal spitting out what I fed him. I tried all sorts of different purées, some with just one or two lumps, but he always picked

them out and often became distressed. By nine months, he was still not eating lumps and I was tearing my hair out because I knew how important it was for him to chew.

Eventually I solved the problem by giving him a little tray of finger foods, including some foods that I went on to purée. This did the trick. He was happy to feed himself lumpy, textured food, but he didn't want anyone messing with his purées. "

FOOD FOR LITTLE FINGERS

Offering finger foods is an ideal way of introducing new textures, tastes, and nutrients, and is also the perfect way to encourage self-feeding.

Begin by introducing foods that melt in your baby's mouth, moving on to foods that require biting when teeth emerge, or when he manages them easily. Good, safe first finger foods are those that can be crushed between your thumb and first finger.

1 Melt in the mouth
Steamed-until-soft vegetables and fruit
Offer carrot sticks, mini broccoli florets, and pieces of apple.

Very ripe fruit
Sometimes fruit is easier to hold when it is left unpeeled because it is less slippery. Soft fruits such as pears, peaches, and nectarines are fine unpeeled. Cut a small banana in half and trim the skin back at the base so that the top sticks out unpeeled and the skin works as a handle. Peel avocado, melon, and mango and cut into wedges. Always cut grapes in half. Leave soft berry fruits such as raspberries and strawberries whole, unless they are very large ones.

Melt-in-the-mouth baby snacks
There are many melt-in-the-mouth, salt-free baby snacks available to buy, such as sweetcorn ring puffs, baked corn and carrot puffs, and miniature rice cakes. These will soon become firm favourites.

2 Bite and dissolve
Potatoes and sweet potatoes
Small pieces of boiled or steamed potato and sweet potato will be easy for your baby to hold. Sweet potato, especially, is packed with nutrients – bake it with the skin on.

Breads
Why not offer a little pitta bread, a chunk of thin bagel, toast, or sultana bread? Cut the bread into fingers or chunks, but avoid crusty breads that can break off and damage your baby's gums, or cause choking. Try sandwiches made with mashed banana, cream cheese, and pure fruit spread.

carrot

bread

apple and pear

"Look — I can feed myself!"

Eating when out and about just got a whole lot easier!

3 Bite and chew

Cucumber sticks and lightly steamed vegetables

Cucumber sticks, as well as steamed carrot sticks, are popular with babies because they are easy to hold. Steamed broccoli and cauliflower florets work – leave the stalk on so it can act as a handle. Chilled cucumber sticks help to soothe sore gums when teething.

Cheese

Cheese is a healthy source of fat and an excellent source of protein. Avoid very hard cheeses, which could cause your baby to choke.

Dried fruit

Good choices are apricots, figs, apple rings, and mango. Dried fruit is a great source of iron and vitamin C. It does, however, contain lots of natural sugars. Try to look for unsulphured fruit, which does not use sulphur dioxide in the drying process. Avoid dried berries.

Mini meatballs, croquettes, and balls

Babies love food that they can pick up and fit neatly into their mouths. Try flavourful meatballs and the various croquettes and balls in the recipe section, such as Sweet Potato and Kale Croquettes (see page 90) and Salmon, Squash, and Kale Balls (see page 105).

Fruit

Once your baby has mastered biting and chewing, you no longer need to steam pieces of fruit. You can now introduce berries too. Berries are "superfoods", which means they contain fantastic levels of nutrients essential for optimum health.

Pasta

Cooked pasta is a great food for your baby to explore. You can buy pasta created from various grains, such as quinoa, wheat, and corn, and these can boost your baby's nutrient intake. If he can't eat gluten, offer rice or buckwheat pasta shapes.

Food for Little Fingers

dried apple

cucumber

pasta

ANNABEL'S TOP 10 WEANING TIPS

Weaning isn't always a straightforward process, as babies have minds of their own – and very distinctive tastes, too! Just when you think you've got it cracked, your baby can suddenly develop eating patterns that leave you anxious and concerned. The good news is that there's a solution for everything. Bear these 10 simple tips in mind and you'll soon have your baby enjoying mealtimes and on course for a lifetime of healthy, happy eating!

1 To avoid your baby becoming a fussy eater, try not to offer her the same purées again and again. Introduce plenty of variety, and if your little one digs in her heels, try mixing new foods with old favourites, until they become familiar.

2 Babies sleep better at night if their tummies are full and they are given foods that keep them satisfied for a longer period of time. It is therefore important for them to have a balanced meal at night that contains protein, which takes longer to digest than carbohydrates. Some protein-rich foods, such as eggs, dairy products, fish, and poultry have the added benefit of being naturally high in tryptophan, which may also help to improve sleep.

3 Babies need proportionately more fat in their diet than adults so it's important to introduce food such as meat, chicken, and cheese from six months and not give only fruit and vegetable purées. Cook with healthy oils such as rapeseed and olive oil. Nut butters and sauces made with whole milk dairy products are also good. Don't give low-fat dairy products.

4 If your baby is putting on excessive weight , make sure you aren't pressing her to eat past the point that she wants to. Babies are born with an innate ability to self-regulate food intake and

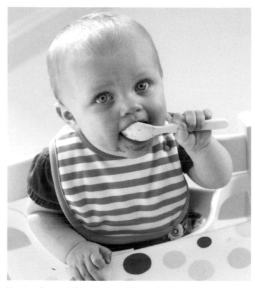

I'm in charge! Don't worry if your baby makes a mess – this is all part of learning to feed herself and also a lot of fun!

no baby needs to clear their bowl. Consider cutting down milk feeds if your baby is getting more than 600ml (1 pint) per day, and speak to your doctor or healthcare provider.

5 Allow your baby to make a mess! Not only will she enjoy eating more, but she'll also be more likely to experiment with different foods, thus developing independent eating habits.

6 If your baby is reluctant to try new foods, hide them in more familiar ones. For example, you can try mixing foods such as spinach or meat with sweet-tasting root vegetables. It's also good to combine savoury and sweet foods such as chicken, sweet potato, and apple. Another way to introduce new foods is as finger foods, as your baby will play with them and put them in her mouth out of curiosity. Remember, it can take many attempts before she accepts a new food.

7 Go at your baby's pace. She may enjoy new foods and consistencies one day but turn her nose up the next. She may also be hungrier some days than others. Try to introduce new foods when she's happy and stick to favourites when she's grumpy. If she doesn't take quickly to new textures, lumps, or chunks, don't panic. Try some of the tips suggested in this book, and relax.

8 Make every effort to make mealtimes a positive experience for your baby. If she senses anxiety or disapproval, she'll find the experience daunting and upsetting. Praise her often, laugh, sing, and show delight at her achievements. Join her by eating a little of what she's having and she'll feel part of the family, too, and begin to associate eating with happy times.

9 Never leave your baby alone when she's eating, as she can choke on even the tiniest piece of food (see page 80). Not only that, but keeping your baby company while she's eating will teach her that eating is a sociable experience, and one to be enjoyed.

10 Plan ahead and freeze batches of foods in ice-cube trays or small pots so you don't need to cook every day.

WHAT SHOULD MY BABY BE DRINKING?

First and foremost, it's important to remember that your baby's tummy is small and if she fills up on milk or water at mealtimes, she's unlikely to eat very much. It's a good idea to get your baby used to drinking from a cup, so try offering some of her normal milk feeds from a beaker (express a little, if you are breastfeeding), and offer water in a beaker between feeds or meals.

Offer your baby water or milk at the end of a meal – these are the only drinks babies need. If you do offer juices, dilute them well and limit them to mealtimes to protect your baby's emerging teeth. Fruit juices mustn't be given full strength as they will fill a baby up with sugar and little else.

Don't give your baby tea to drink as it contains tannins that can hinder essential iron absorption.

Alongside this milk and water, your baby will still need her usual milk feeds, which provide her with the nutrients she needs to grow and develop.

Annabel's Top 10 Weaning Tips

You don't need to buy special baby cereals. Porridge makes an excellent breakfast for your baby and you can sweeten it with fruit purées, such as apple or pear, or stir in a mashed banana, or try this delicious porridge, made with fresh berries. You can use whole cow's milk with cereal and in cooking once your baby is six months old, but continue to use breast or formula as your baby's main milk.

PURPLE PORRIDGE

❄ **Not suitable for freezing**

Makes 1 portion • Suitable from 20 weeks • Prep time 1 minute • Cooking time 5 minutes • Provides energy, calcium, protein, iron, soluble fibre

20g (³/₄oz) porridge oats
150ml (5fl oz) whole milk or a suitable dairy-free formula milk for under 12 months or almond milk for over 12 months
30g (1oz) raspberries
30g (1oz) blueberries
½ tsp maple syrup (optional)

1 Measure the oats and milk into a small saucepan. Stir over a medium heat until boiling, then lower the heat. Simmer for 2 minutes, until the oats are tender.

2 Add the berries and simmer for another 2 minutes until the fruits have softened. Serve with maple syrup, if using.

To add iron to this recipe, add two stoned and chopped soft dates to the oats and milk in step 1.

A good way to introduce green vegetables, such as broccoli, is to mix them with sweet-tasting root vegetables.

SWEET POTATO WITH BROCCOLI AND PEAS

❄ **Suitable for freezing**

Makes 4 portions • Suitable from 6 months • Prep time 5 minutes • Cooking time 14 minutes
• Provides energy, fibre, vitamin C, vitamin A

1 sweet potato (about 450g/1lb), peeled and diced

2 broccoli florets (about 55g/2oz), halved

3 tbsp frozen peas

1 Steam the sweet potato for 6 minutes. Add the broccoli and steam for a further 4 minutes, then add the peas and steam for 4 minutes more.

2 Purée in a food processor or put in a bowl and use a hand-blender, adding enough water from the steamer to make a smooth consistency, or mash with a knob of butter and splash of milk.

3 Freeze in individual portions. When needed, thaw overnight in the fridge or for 1–2 hours at room temperature, then microwave or reheat in a small pan until piping hot. Stir and allow to cool before serving.

Not only is this deliciously smooth purée highly nutritious, but it also has a sweet, mild flavour that your baby will love.

PUMPKIN AND PEA PURÉE

❄ **Suitable for freezing**

Makes 4 portions • Suitable from 6 months • Prep time 10 minutes • Cooking time 17 minutes
• Provides protein, fibre, vitamin A

15g (1/2oz) unsalted butter or dairy-free spread

2.5cm (1in) piece leek, thinly sliced

250g (9oz) peeled and diced pumpkin

120ml (4fl oz) unsalted vegetable stock or water

3 tbsp frozen peas

1 Melt the butter in a saucepan and sauté the leek gently, stirring, for 3 minutes, or until softened.

2 Add the pumpkin and cook gently for 1 minute. Pour over the stock or water, bring to the boil, reduce the heat, cover, and simmer for 10 minutes. Add the peas and cook for 3 minutes. Purée in a food processor or use a hand-blender.

3 Freeze in individual portions. Thaw overnight in the fridge or for 1–2 hours at room temperature, then microwave or reheat in a small pan until piping hot. Stir and allow to cool before serving.

Root vegetables, such as potatoes and carrots, are firm favourites with babies, and the fruitiness of sweetcorn makes this purée irresistible.

POTATO, CARROT, AND SWEETCORN

❄ **Suitable for freezing**
Makes 4 portions • Suitable from 6 months • Prep time 10 minutes • Cooking time 18 minutes • Provides fibre, vitamin A, vitamin B1 • Dairy-free

1 tbsp olive oil
½ small onion, peeled and chopped
1 medium carrot, peeled and sliced
1 large potato, peeled and diced
150ml (5fl oz) unsalted vegetable stock or water
3 tbsp sweetcorn, frozen or canned without sugar or salt

1 Heat the oil and sauté the onion and carrot gently for 5 minutes, stirring.

2 Add the potato, pour over the stock or water, and bring to the boil. Cover, reduce the heat, and simmer for 10 minutes, or until tender. Add the sweetcorn and cook for a further 3 minutes.

3 Purée in a baby food grinder or mouli or place in a bowl and use a hand-blender.

4 Freeze in individual portions. When needed, thaw overnight in the fridge or for 1–2 hours at room temperature, then microwave or reheat in a small pan until piping hot. Stir and allow to cool before serving.

For baby-led weaning, see the recipe opposite.

EXPLORING NEW TASTES AND TEXTURES // Stage Two – 6 to 9 months

Using more or less the same ingredients as in the recipe on the opposite page, you can make these delicious veggie balls, which are perfect for baby-led weaning.

POTATO, CARROT, AND SWEETCORN BALLS

✳ **Suitable for freezing**

Makes 18 • Suitable from 24 weeks • Prep time 15–20 minutes • Cooking time 20 minutes
• Provides energy, calcium, vitamin A, fibre

1 medium carrot, peeled and sliced

1 medium potato, peeled and diced

½ onion, peeled and chopped

1 tsp freshly chopped thyme

70g (2½oz) fresh breadcrumbs or wheat- or gluten-free breadcrumbs

30g (1oz) Cheddar cheese or dairy-free alternative, grated

½ tsp sweet chilli sauce

3 tbsp tinned sweetcorn, frozen or canned without sugar or salt

Plain flour or gluten-free flour

1 tbsp sunflower oil

1 Place the carrot and potato in a steamer and steam for 15 minutes until soft. Leave to cool.

2 Place the remaining ingredients except the flour and oil into a food processor. Whizz together until finely chopped. Shape into 18 balls and roll in the flour.

3 Heat the oil in a frying pan. Fry the balls for 5–6 minutes over a medium heat, until golden on all sides and heated through.

4 When needed, thaw overnight in the fridge or for a few hours at room temperature. Reheat in an oven preheated to 180°C (fan 160°C), gas 4 for about 10 minutes.

Flex it...

Use a medium parsnip instead of carrot for added sweetness.

Potato, Carrot, and Sweetcorn Balls

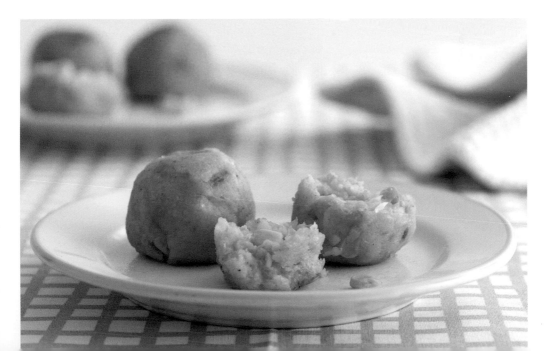

Most babies are open to trying new foods. However, it can be tricky getting them to enjoy eating leafy green vegetables, so that's why I've created these super-tasty veggie croquettes. Kale is such a bona fide superfood that it would be hard to find a reason to keep it off your child's menu.

SWEET POTATO AND KALE CROQUETTES

❄ **Suitable for freezing**

Makes 14 • Suitable from 26 weeks • Prep time 15 minutes • Cooking time 9–10 minutes (2 batches) • Provides energy, calcium, protein, vitamin A, vitamin K, several minerals

2 tbsp sunflower oil

1 small onion, chopped

100g (3½oz) mushrooms, chopped

1 medium carrot, grated

20g (¾oz) kale, chopped

1 garlic clove, crushed

150g (5½oz) baking potato, pricked

150g (5½oz) sweet potato, pricked

50g (1¾oz) fresh breadcrumbs or wheat- or gluten-free breadcrumbs

30g (1oz) Cheddar cheese or dairy-free alternative, grated

Plain flour or gluten-free flour, to coat

1 Heat 1 tablespoon of the oil in a frying pan. Add the onion, mushrooms, carrot, kale, and garlic, and fry for 5 minutes over a medium heat. Leave to cool.

2 Cook the potatoes in a microwave for 10 minutes until soft. Leave to cool, then scoop out the potato flesh into a bowl.

3 Add the cooked vegetables, breadcrumbs, and cheese and mix together until blended. Shape into 14 small croquettes and roll in the flour.

4 Heat the remaining 1 tablespoon of oil in a frying pan. Fry the croquettes for 3–4 minutes, until golden on all sides and cooked through. Drain on kitchen paper and leave to cool before serving.

5 When needed, thaw overnight in the fridge or leave out for a few hours at room temperature. Reheat in an oven preheated to 180°C (fan 160°C), gas 4 for 10–12 minutes.

Flex it...

If you don't have kale, you can use other nutritious greens such as cabbage or Swiss chard.

Replace the mushrooms with red pepper for added beta-carotene.

Tofu, or soya bean curd, is a high-protein superfood containing calcium, iron, and zinc. Combine it with flour, vegetables, and Parmesan cheese to make these tasty croquettes that are a perfect finger food.

VEGETABLE AND TOFU CROQUETTES

❄ **Suitable for freezing**

Makes 12 croquettes • Suitable from 28 weeks • Prep time 10 minutes • Cooking time 20 minutes • Provides energy, protein, calcium, vitamin A, iron, zinc

350g (12oz) jacket potato, pricked

50g (1³/₄oz) butternut squash, grated

50g (1³/₄oz) courgette, grated

75g (2½oz) firm tofu

50g (1³/₄oz) mushrooms, chopped

30g (1oz) Parmesan cheese or dairy-free alternative, grated

50g (1³/₄oz) cream crackers or wheat- or gluten-free alternative

Plain flour or gluten-free flour, for coating

Sunflower oil

1 Cook the potato in a microwave for 10 to 12 minutes until soft. Leave to cool, then scoop out the middle into a bowl. (If you have more time, you can prick the potato and bake it in an oven preheated to 200°C (fan 180°C), gas 6 for about 45 minutes or until tender.

2 Combine the remaining ingredients, except the flour and oil, in a bowl. Lightly season and then shape into 12 croquettes. Roll the croquettes in the flour.

3 Heat a little oil in a frying pan. Fry for 5 to 6 minutes until lightly golden. Drain on kitchen paper and leave to cool before serving.

4 Freeze the croquettes after cooking them. When needed, thaw overnight in the fridge or leave out a few hours at room temperature. Reheat in an oven preheated to 180°C (fan 160°C), gas 4 for 10–12 minutes.

Flex it...

Replace the butternut squash with another winter squash such as pumpkin. Or use turnip, a root vegetable that is loaded with immune-boosting vitamin C.

If you don't have Parmesan cheese to hand, replace with Cheddar.

EXPLORING NEW TASTES AND TEXTURES // Stage Two – 6 to 9 months

Unless you are bringing your baby up on a vegetarian diet, it is important to introduce red meat from 6 months as your baby's iron stores become depleted at this age and red meat provides the best and most easily absorbed source of iron. This tasty recipe also has the advantage of being dairy free.

TASTY VEGGIE-MINCE WITH PASTA

❄ **Suitable for freezing**

Makes 8 portions • Suitable from 28 weeks • Prep time 10 minutes • Cooking time 40 minutes
• Provides energy, protein, fibre, vitamin C • Dairy-free

2 tsp sunflower oil
1 onion, finely diced
½ red pepper, diced
½ courgette, diced
6 button mushrooms, diced
250g (9oz) lean minced beef
1 garlic clove, crushed
400g can chopped
   tomatoes
2 tbsp tomato purée
2 tbsp freshly chopped basil
150g (5½oz) orzo pasta or
   wheat- or gluten-free
   orzo pasta

1 Heat the oil in a saucepan. Add the onion, red pepper, courgette, and mushrooms, and fry over a high heat for 5 minutes.

2 Add the beef and continue to fry until browned. Add the garlic and fry for 10 seconds.

3 Add the tomatoes, tomato purée, and basil. Cover and simmer over a low heat for 30 minutes until tender.

4 Cook the orzo in boiling water according to the packet instructions. Meanwhile, drain and mix with the veggie-mince sauce.

5 Freeze in individual portions. When needed, thaw overnight in the fridge or leave out for a few hours at room temperature. Reheat in a saucepan, stirring over a medium heat for about 5 minutes, until heated through.

Flex it...

Replace the beef with the equivalent amount of minced beef or chicken.

If you don't have orzo, use any other small variety of pasta.

Tasty Veggie-Mince with Pasta

Adding cheese to your baby's purées is an excellent way to ensure a concentrated source of energy that will help fuel rapid growth in your baby's first year. This tasty purée is bursting with autumn flavours.

CHEESY LEEK, SWEET POTATO, AND CAULIFLOWER

❄ **Suitable for freezing**

Makes 4 portions • Suitable from 6 months • Prep time 5 minutes • Cooking time 13 minutes • Provides energy, protein, calcium, vitamin A

10g (¹/₄oz) unsalted butter or dairy-free alternative

5cm (2in) piece of leek, sliced

¹/₂ small sweet potato, peeled and diced (about 150g/5¹/₂oz)

250ml (8fl oz) boiling water

2 good-sized cauliflower florets, cut into small pieces

30g (1oz) Cheddar cheese or dairy-free alternative, grated

1 Heat the butter in a pan and add the leek. Sauté gently for about 3 minutes until softened.

2 Add the sweet potato, pour over the boiling water, bring back to the boil, and cook for 5 minutes. Add the cauliflower, reduce the heat to moderate, cover, and continue to cook for another 5 minutes.

3 Purée the contents of the pan in a food processor together with the grated cheese.

4 Freeze in individual portions. Thaw overnight in the fridge or for 1–2 hours at room temperature, then microwave or reheat in a small pan until piping hot. Stir and allow to cool before serving.

You may be surprised to hear that lentil purées are some of my most popular baby recipes. Lentils are an excellent source of protein and iron, and they also contain fibre. What's more, babies love them!

LENTIL PURÉE WITH SWEET POTATO

❄ **Suitable for freezing**

Makes 3 portions • Suitable from 6 months • Prep time 10 minutes • Cooking time 30 minutes
• Provides energy, protein, soluble fibre, vitamin A, vitamin C • Dairy-free

1 tbsp sunflower oil

1 small onion, peeled and chopped

¼ red pepper, cored, deseeded, and chopped

1 medium tomato, skinned (see tip, below), deseeded, and roughly chopped

2 tbsp red lentils

½ small sweet potato, peeled and diced (about 150g/5½oz)

200ml (7fl oz) unsalted vegetable stock or water

1 Heat the oil in a pan and sauté the onion and red pepper gently, stirring, for 4 minutes until softened. Add the tomato and sauté, stirring, for 1 minute.

2 Rinse the lentils, add them to the pan along with the sweet potato, and pour over the vegetable stock or water. Bring to the boil, reduce the heat, cover, and simmer for 20–25 minutes, or until the lentils are quite mushy. Top up with a little more water if necessary, but there should be only a little liquid left in the pan at the end.

3 Purée until smooth in a food processor or place in a bowl and use a hand-blender.

4 Freeze in individual portions. When needed, thaw overnight in the fridge or for 1–2 hours at room temperature, then microwave or reheat in a small pan until piping hot. Stir and allow to cool before serving.

Tip: To peel tomatoes, as well as other thick-skinned fruits, cut a shallow cross on the bottom with a small, sharp knife. Place the fruit in a bowl, cover with boiling water, then leave for 30–60 seconds. Drain and rinse in cold water. When the fruit is cool enough to handle, find the cross you made. Grasp a corner of loose skin and gently pull off the skin.

Rich, sweet, and full of antioxidants and other nutrients, this creamy pasta dish will appeal to babies and children of all ages. You can freeze the sauce separately in individual portions then thaw, reheat, and add to freshly cooked pasta before serving if you prefer.

TOMATO AND BUTTERNUT SQUASH PASTA

❄ **Suitable for freezing**

Makes 5 portions • Suitable from 6 months • Prep time 10 minutes • Cooking time 40 minutes • Provides energy, protein, vitamin A, fibre

2 tsp light olive oil

½ small red onion, peeled and finely chopped

1 tsp fresh chopped thyme or ¼ tsp dried thyme

125g (4½oz) peeled and diced butternut squash

1 garlic clove, peeled and crushed

400g (14oz) can chopped tomatoes

75ml (5 tbsp) water

½ tsp sun-dried tomato paste or tomato purée

30g (1oz) Cheddar cheese or dairy-free alternative, grated

1 tbsp double cream or dairy-free alternative

75g (2½oz) conchigliette (baby pasta shells) or wheat- or gluten-free pasta

1 Heat the oil in a saucepan. Add the onion, thyme, and butternut squash. Sauté, stirring, over a low heat for 5 minutes. Add the garlic and cook for a further 1 minute.

2 Add the remaining ingredients except the cheese and cream. Bring to the boil, reduce the heat, and simmer gently for 30 minutes or until soft and pulpy, stirring occasionally.

3 Add the cheese and purée the mixture until smooth in a food processor or place in a bowl and use a hand-blender. Mix in the cream.

4 Meanwhile cook the pasta in boiling water according to the packet directions, then drain, and stir in the tomato and butternut squash sauce before serving.

5 Freeze in individual portions. When needed, thaw overnight in the fridge or for 1–2 hours at room temperature, then microwave or reheat in a small pan until piping hot. Stir and allow to cool before serving.

Flex it...

Replace the thyme with the same quantity of dried or fresh basil, which is considered to be one of the healthiest herbs.

Tasty pasta. Pasta dishes can be flexed with a wide range of foods to introduce your baby to different flavours and textures.

This nourishing chowder makes a perfect meal for a hungry baby.
In fact, the whole family will enjoy the rich, delicious flavours.

SALMON AND CORN CHOWDER

❄ **Suitable for freezing**

Makes 5 portions • Suitable from 6 months • Prep time 10 minutes • Cooking time 20 minutes
• Provides energy, protein, omega-3 EFAs, fibre, vitamin D, vitamin B$_{12}$

1 tbsp olive oil

1 small onion, peeled and chopped

2 medium carrots, peeled and diced

½ stick celery, strings removed (see tip, below) and chopped

1 medium potato, peeled and diced

1 small garlic clove, peeled and crushed

100ml (3½fl oz) unsalted vegetable stock or water

100ml (3½fl oz) whole milk or a suitable dairy-free formula milk for under 12 months or almond milk for over 12 months

115g (4oz) boneless salmon fillet, skinned and cut into small cubes

100g (3½oz) canned sweetcorn (with no added sugar or salt) packed in water, drained

1 Heat the oil in a saucepan. Stir in the onion, carrot, celery, and potato. Reduce the heat as low as possible, cover, and cook very gently for 10 minutes, stirring occasionally. Add the garlic and stir for 30 seconds.

2 Add the stock or water, bring to the boil, cover, and cook for 8 minutes until tender. Add the milk, salmon, and sweetcorn, bring back to the boil, reduce the heat again, and cook gently for a further 4 minutes.

3 Purée until smooth in a food processor or place in a bowl and use a hand-blender. For older babies, mash with a fork.

4 Freeze in individual portions. When needed, thaw overnight in the fridge or for 1–2 hours at room temperature, then microwave or reheat in a small pan until piping hot. Stir and allow to cool before serving.

Tip:

The easy way to remove strings from celery is to peel the sticks with a potato peeler. This prevents unpleasant strands appearing in the finished dish.

Flex it...

Replace the carrots with the same quantity of courgettes, which are packed with immune-boosting vitamin C.

Use a sweet potato – they contain more fibre and vitamin A than a standard white potato.

It's hard to find a jar of baby purée that contains oily fish such as salmon, yet the essential fatty acids in oily fish are particularly important for the development of your baby's brain, nervous system, and vision, and ideally should be included in his diet twice a week. Did you know that fats such as these are also one of the principal sources of calories in breast milk?

POACHED SALMON WITH CARROTS AND PEAS

❄ **Suitable for freezing**

Makes 3 portions • Suitable from 6 months • Prep time 8 minutes • Cooking time 11 minutes • Provides energy, protein, omega-3 EFAs, fibre, vitamin D, vitamin B$_{12}$

150ml (5fl oz) unsalted vegetable stock or water

1 small potato, peeled and diced

1 medium carrot, peeled and diced

100g (3½oz) boneless salmon fillet, skinned and cut into small cubes

2 tbsp frozen peas

45g (1½oz) Cheddar cheese or dairy-free alternative, grated

1 Put the stock or water in a saucepan with the potato and carrot. Bring to the boil, then cook over a moderate heat for 7–8 minutes, or until the potato and carrot are just tender.

2 Add the salmon and peas. Cover again and simmer for 3 minutes, until the fish flakes easily and the vegetables are tender. Remove from the heat and stir in the grated cheese.

3 Purée until smooth in a food processor or place in a bowl and use a hand-blender. For older babies, mash with a fork.

4 Freeze in individual portions. When needed, thaw overnight in the fridge or for 1–2 hours at room temperature, then microwave or reheat in a small pan until piping hot. Stir and allow to cool before serving.

Flex it...

Replace the salmon with the same quantity of cod or pollock, which is also a source of omega-3 fatty acids.

Use the same quantity of frozen mixed vegetables in place of the peas.

White fish such as cod is an excellent source of high-value protein. The cheese and milk in this dish provide calcium, which is essential to bone health. You can add a little less milk to this recipe if you are making it for an older baby.

COD WITH BUTTERNUT SQUASH AND CHEESE SAUCE

❄ **Suitable for freezing**

Makes 4 portions • Suitable from 28 weeks • Prep time 10 minutes • Cooking time 11 minutes • Provides energy, calcium, vitamin B12, vitamin A, protein

15g (½oz) unsalted butter or dairy-free spread

½ small onion, peeled and finely chopped

85g (3oz) peeled and diced butternut squash

15g (½oz) plain flour or gluten-free flour

75ml (5 tbsp) whole milk or a suitable dairy-free formula milk for under 12 months or almond milk for over 12 months

75ml (5 tbsp) unsalted vegetable stock or water

100g (3½oz) cod fillet, skinned and cut into small cubes

30g (1oz) Parmesan cheese or dairy-free alternative, freshly grated

1 Melt the butter in a saucepan and stir in the onion and butternut squash. Reduce the heat as low as possible, cover, and cook very gently for 5 minutes until soft, stirring occasionally.

2 Stir in the flour and cook for 1 minute. Remove from the heat, gradually add the milk and stock or water, return to the heat, bring to the boil, and simmer for 2 minutes, stirring.

3 Add the cubes of fish and cook for 2–3 minutes, until tender and cooked through.

4 Add the cheese and purée the mixture until smooth in a food processor or place in a bowl and use a hand-blender. For older babies, mash with a fork.

5 Freeze in individual portions. Thaw overnight in the fridge or for 1–2 hours at room temperature, then microwave or reheat in a small pan until piping hot. Stir and allow to cool before serving.

For baby-led weaning, place the cod fillet on a piece of foil with a knob of butter, wrap it up as a parcel, and bake in the oven at 180°C (fan 160°C), gas 4 for about 15 minutes. Once cooled, your baby can pick up and eat the perfectly cooked pieces of cod. Serve with some steamed vegetables, such as broccoli. See also the recipe on the opposite page.

Flex it...

Replace the cod with plaice or hake, which are equally nutritious.

Use any winter squash in place of the butternut.

If you've chosen the baby-led weaning route, you can take the same ingredients as for the recipe opposite, add some fresh sage and a little sweet chilli, and whizz everything together to make these tasty croquettes.

COD AND SQUASH CROQUETTES

❄ **Suitable for freezing**

Makes 10 • Suitable from 28 weeks • Prep time 10 minutes • Cooking time 8 minutes
• Provides energy, protein, vitamin A, calcium

½ onion, diced

85g (3oz) peeled and grated butternut squash

100g (3½oz) cod fillet, skinned and cut into small cubes

30g (1oz) Parmesan cheese or dairy-free alternative, grated

70g (2½oz) breadcrumbs or gluten-free breadcrumbs

1 tsp sweet chilli sauce

1 tsp freshly chopped sage

Plain flour or gluten-free flour

1 tbsp sunflower oil, for frying

1 Place all the ingredients except the flour and oil in a food processor. Whizz until finely chopped. Shape into 10 croquette shapes and roll in the flour.

2 Heat the oil in a frying pan. Fry the croquettes for 10–12 minutes over a medium heat, until golden on all sides and cooked through. Drain on kitchen paper and leave to cool before serving.

3 When needed, thaw overnight in the fridge or leave out for a few hours at room temperature. Reheat in an oven preheated to 180°C (fan 160°C), gas 4 for 10–12 minutes.

Cod and Squash Croquettes

This flavourful fish purée is packed with protein and vitamins, making it the perfect way to make sure your baby gets the nutrients she needs. Miss out the puréeing stage and top with mashed potatoes for a delicious family fish pie.

SPINACH AND COD PURÉE

❄ **Suitable for freezing**

Makes 3 portions • Suitable from 6 months • Prep time 8 minutes • Cooking time 16 minutes • Provides energy, protein, calcium, vitamin K, vitamin B12

15g (½oz) unsalted butter or dairy-free spread

5cm (2in) piece of leek, finely sliced

1 medium potato, peeled and diced

100ml (3½fl oz) unsalted vegetable stock or water

75ml (5 tbsp) whole milk or a suitable dairy-free formula milk for under 12 months or almond milk for over 12 months

2 handfuls baby spinach leaves, roughly chopped

100g (3½oz) boneless cod fillet or other white fish, skinned and cut into small cubes

15g (½oz) Parmesan cheese or dairy-free alternative, freshly grated

1 Heat the butter in a saucepan. Add the leek and sauté gently, stirring, for 3 minutes. Add the potato and sauté, stirring, for 2 minutes.

2 Add the stock or water and milk. Bring to the boil, reduce the heat, cover, and simmer for 8 minutes, until the vegetables are tender.

3 Add the spinach and cod and stir over the heat for 3 minutes, or until the spinach has wilted and the cod is cooked. Stir in the cheese and purée until smooth in a food processor or place in a bowl and use a hand-blender. For older babies, mash with a fork.

4 Freeze in individual portions. When needed, thaw overnight in the fridge or for 1–2 hours at room temperature, then microwave or reheat in a small pan until piping hot. Stir and allow to cool before serving.

Flex it...

Use Swiss chard instead of spinach. This nutrient-rich vegetable is a great source of vitamins K, A, and C.

It's never too early to establish oily fish on the menu, and this salmon purée provides lots of EFAs to encourage healthy growth and development.

ANNABEL'S TASTY SALMON

❄ **Suitable for freezing**

Makes 2 portions • Suitable from 6 months • Prep time 5 minutes • Cooking time 15 minutes • Provides protein, omega-3 EFAs, vitamin D, vitamin B12, vitamin A

1 large carrot, peeled and diced

100g (3½oz) boneless salmon fillet, skinned

1 tbsp whole milk or a suitable dairy-free formula milk for under 12 months or almond milk for over 12 months

15g (½oz) unsalted butter or dairy-free spread

2 good-sized ripe tomatoes, skinned (see tip, page 95), deseeded, and roughly chopped

30g (1oz) Cheddar cheese or dairy-free alternative, grated

1 Steam the carrot for 15 minutes or until tender.

2 Put the salmon in a small microwaveable dish, add the milk, cover with cling film rolled back at one edge, and microwave for 1½ minutes, until the fish is just opaque. Leave to stand – it will continue cooking.

3 Melt the butter in a saucepan and sauté the tomatoes, stirring until pulpy (about 3 minutes). Remove from the heat and stir in the grated cheese until melted.

4 Flake the fish and mix this together with the tomato and cheese sauce and the steamed carrot. If your baby isn't ready for lumps yet, whizz the mixture in the food processor.

5 Freeze in individual portions. Thaw overnight in the fridge or for 1–2 hours at room temperature, then microwave or reheat in a small pan until piping hot. Stir and allow to cool before serving.

For baby-led weaning, place the salmon on a piece of foil with a knob of butter, wrap up as a parcel, and bake at 180°C (fan 160°C), gas 4 for about 15 minutes. Your baby can then eat the perfectly cooked pieces of salmon.

Ideally, you should give your baby oily fish twice a week. A baby's brain triples in size during the first year and the omega-3s in oily fish are very important for the development of your child's brain and vision. Try these tasty, power-packed salmon balls, which also have the advantage of being dairy-free.

SALMON, SQUASH, AND KALE BALLS

❄ **Suitable for freezing**

Makes 20 • Suitable from 6 months • Prep time 15 minutes • Cooking time 15–18 minutes • Provides energy, protein, vitamin D, vitamin A, omega-3 EFAs, vitamin K • Dairy-free

50g (1³/₄oz) kale, trimmed
50g (1³/₄oz) fresh brown breadcrumbs or wheat- or gluten-free breadcrumbs
3 spring onions, chopped
1 tbsp freshly chopped dill
100g (3¹/₂oz) butternut squash, peeled and grated
250g (9oz) salmon fillet, skinned and diced
1 tbsp tomato ketchup
1 tsp soy sauce
Squeeze of fresh lemon juice

1 Preheat the oven to 200°C (fan 180°C), gas 6. Line a baking sheet with non-stick paper.

2 Cook the kale in a pan of boiling water for 3 minutes. Drain and refresh under cold running water. Drain well and squeeze out the water. Roughly chop.

3 Place all the remaining ingredients in a food processor with the kale. Whizz until finely chopped. Don't add salt for babies under one year, but lightly season for toddlers over one.

4 Shape into 20 balls using wet hands and place on the baking tray. Bake for 12–15 minutes, until lightly golden and firm underneath. Alternatively, sauté in 2 tablespoons sunflower oil for 8–10 minutes, drain on kitchen paper, and leave to cool before serving.

5 When needed, thaw overnight in the fridge or leave out for a few hours at room temperature. Reheat in an oven preheated to 180°C (fan 160°C), gas 4 for 10–12 minutes.

Flex it...

Use 2 tablespoons of snipped chives instead of the spring onions.

Salmon, Squash, and Kale Balls

You will be amazed at some of the flavours that will appeal to your baby, so do introduce mild spices to add variety to her diet. Butternut squash is a fantastic source of beta-carotene, which your baby's body converts into vitamin A, essential for his developing vision and immune system.

MILD CHICKEN AND APRICOT CURRY

❄ **Suitable for freezing**

Makes 3–4 portions • Suitable from 28 weeks • Prep time 10 minutes • Cooking time 17 minutes • Provides energy, fibre, protein, vitamin A, iron • Dairy-free

1 tbsp sunflower oil

1 small onion, peeled and chopped

¼ tsp fresh ginger, grated (optional)

1½ tsp mild curry paste, such as Korma

100ml (3½fl oz) unsalted chicken stock or water

100ml (3½fl oz) coconut milk

4 dried apricots, roughly chopped

¼ small butternut squash, peeled and finely diced (about 150g/5½oz)

1 small chicken breast, cut into small cubes

1 Heat the oil in a saucepan. Add the onion and ginger, if using, and sauté gently, stirring for 5 minutes. Add the curry paste and fry, stirring for 30 seconds.

2 Add the remaining ingredients, bring to the boil, reduce the heat, cover, and simmer for about 12 minutes, until the squash is tender and the chicken is cooked through.

3 Purée until smooth in a food processor or place in a bowl and use a hand-blender. For older babies chop in a food processor or by hand to the desired consistency.

4 Freeze in individual portions. Thaw overnight in the fridge or for 1–2 hours at room temperature, then microwave or reheat in a small pan until piping hot. Stir and allow to cool before serving.

For baby-led weaning, see the recipe on the opposite page.

This is a great baby-led alternative to the curry on the opposite page. The mild fruitiness of the apricots and the creamy coconut milk add new flavours.

CHICKEN CURRY STRIPS WITH CURRY SAUCE

Not suitable for freezing

Makes 3 portions • Suitable from 28 weeks • Prep time 10 minutes • Cooking time 32 minutes
• Provides energy, protein, vitamin A, fibre • Dairy-free

1 tsp mild curry paste, such as Korma
1 tsp mango chutney
1/2 tsp sunflower oil
1 chicken breast, sliced into strips

For the curry sauce
1 tbsp sunflower oil
1 small onion, chopped
1/2 apple, grated
1/4 tsp ground ginger
1 1/2 tsp mild curry paste, such as Korma
150ml (5fl oz) unsalted chicken stock
150ml (5fl oz) coconut milk
2 dried apricots, chopped
150g (5 1/2oz) butternut squash, diced

1 Preheat the oven to 200°C (fan 180°C), gas 6. Line a baking sheet with foil.

2 To make the curry sauce, heat the oil in a saucepan. Add the onion, apple, and ginger. Fry for 5 minutes over a medium heat. Add the curry paste and fry for 10 seconds. Add the stock, coconut milk, apricots, and butternut squash.

3 Bring to the boil, then cover and simmer for 15 minutes. Blend until smooth using a hand blender.

4 Meanwhile, mix the curry paste, mango chutney, and oil together. Add the chicken and coat. Arrange on the baking sheet.

5 Bake the chicken in the preheated oven for 10–12 minutes, until browned and cooked through. Once cooled, serve with the curry sauce.

Chicken Curry Strips with Curry Sauce

This is a delicious combination purée, and the addition of garlic and fresh basil works to bring out the natural flavours. It's also full of nutrients, such as vitamin A, fibre, protein, and antioxidants, to encourage healthy growth and development.

CHICKEN WITH SWEET POTATO, PEAS, AND BASIL

❄ **Suitable for freezing**

Makes 5 portions • Suitable from 6 months • Prep time 6 minutes • Cooking time 20 minutes
• Provides energy, protein, fibre, iron, vitamin A, vitamin C • Dairy-free

1½ tbsp olive oil

1 small onion, peeled and chopped

½ small red pepper, deseeded and diced

1 garlic clove, peeled and crushed

1 small chicken breast, cut into small cubes

2 tbsp pure apple juice

175ml (6fl oz) unsalted chicken stock or water

1 medium courgette, diced

½ small sweet potato, peeled and diced (about 150g/5½oz)

4 tbsp frozen peas

6 fresh basil leaves, chopped

1 Heat the olive oil in a saucepan and sauté the onion and red pepper, stirring, for 4 minutes until softened. Add the garlic and sauté for 1 minute.

2 Stir in the chicken and continue to cook for 2–3 minutes, stirring. Pour over the apple juice and stock or water and stir in the courgette and sweet potato. Bring to the boil, cover, reduce the heat, and simmer gently for 8 minutes. Stir in the peas and continue to cook for 3 minutes, until everything is tender and cooked through. Stir in the basil.

3 Purée in a food processor or place in a bowl and use a hand-blender. For older babies, chop in a food processor or by hand to the desired consistency.

4 Freeze in individual portions. When required, thaw overnight in the fridge or for 1–2 hours at room temperature, then microwave or reheat in a small pan until piping hot. Stir and allow to cool before serving.

For baby-led weaning, marinate strips of chicken in 1 tablespoon of olive oil, half a teaspoon of chopped thyme, and half a clove of garlic, bashed, for 15 minutes. Remove from the marinade. Heat 2 teaspoons of sunflower oil in a frying pan and sauté for 2–3 minutes each side. Serve with roasted sweet potato: scrub the sweet potato, but don't peel it. Cut into wedges and arrange on a baking tray. Brush with a little oil and roast for 20–25 minutes at 180°C (fan 160°C), gas 4.

The right consistency.
Gradually make purées
lumpier to get your baby
used to different textures.

Chicken is often a firm favourite with babies, and it blends well with the soft consistency and mild fruitiness of puréed parsnip. If you wish, you can replace the chicken breast with boneless chicken thighs, which are higher in zinc and iron. This easy purée also freezes well.

CHICKEN AND PARSNIP PURÉE

❄ **Suitable for freezing**

Makes 4 portions • Suitable from 6 months • Prep time 8 minutes • Cooking time 15 minutes
• Provides protein, fibre, B vitamins, zinc • Dairy-free

2 tsp sunflower oil
5cm (2in) piece of leek, sliced
1 small chicken breast, cut into small cubes
1 small parsnip, peeled and diced
85g (3oz) butternut squash, peeled and diced
1/2 small apple, peeled and grated
250ml (8fl oz) unsalted chicken stock or water
Good pinch chopped fresh thyme or small pinch dried thyme

1 Heat the oil in a saucepan. Add the leek and sauté gently, stirring, for 3 minutes. Add the chicken and sauté for 2 minutes.

2 Add the remaining ingredients, bring to the boil, cover, reduce the heat, and simmer gently for 8–10 minutes, until all of the vegetables are soft and the chicken is cooked through.

3 Purée until smooth in a food processor or place in a bowl and use a hand-blender. For older babies, chop in a food processor or by hand to the desired consistency.

4 Freeze in individual portions. Thaw overnight in the fridge or for 1–2 hours at room temperature, then microwave or reheat in a small pan until piping hot. Stir and allow to cool before serving.

For baby-led weaning, marinate the chicken for 15 minutes in a tablespoon of olive oil, 1/2 teaspoon chopped thyme, and 1/2 garlic clove, bashed. Then cut into strips and sauté for 2–3 minutes each side in 2 teaspoons of oil. Slice the parsnip into wedges, brush with oil, and bake in a preheated oven at 180°C (fan 160°C), gas 4 for 20 minutes. Alternatively, see the baby-led weaning recipe on the opposite page.

My son wasn't keen on eating chicken until I made mini chicken balls and added some grated apple. Even though he is now in his twenties, we still enjoy eating these Chicken and Apple Balls. These will be loved by all the family.

CHICKEN AND APPLE BALLS

❄ **Suitable for freezing**

Makes 25 • Suitable from 6 months • Prep time 15 minutes • Cooking time 5–15 minutes
 • Provides energy, protein, iron, calcium

500g (1lb 2oz) boneless chicken thighs, diced

1 onion, diced

1 tbsp freshly chopped sage

1 apple, peeled and grated

75g (2½oz) breadcrumbs or wheat- or gluten-free breadcrumbs

40g (1½oz) Parmesan cheese or dairy-free alternative, grated

1½ tsp chopped oregano, thyme, or sage

2 tbsp sunflower oil, for frying

1 Put the chicken into a food processor and whizz until finely chopped. Add the remaining ingredients, apart from the oil, and whizz again until finely chopped. Shape into 25 balls.

2 Heat 1 tablespoon of sunflower oil in a frying pan, add half the chicken balls, and fry over a medium heat for 5 minutes, until lightly golden on all sides and cooked through. Drain on kitchen paper. Add the remaining oil to the pan and cook the second batch of chicken balls in the same way.

3 Alternatively, preheat the oven to 180°C (fan 160°C), gas 4. Arrange the chicken balls on a baking tray lined with non-stick paper and bake for 12–15 minutes.

4 Leave the balls to cool before serving.

5 Freeze in a plastic freezer box. Defrost overnight in the fridge and reheat in the oven (see step 3).

Flex it...

Replace the chicken
with the same amount of turkey or pork and the apple with the same amount of grated pear.

Chicken and Apple Balls

Bulgur wheat is a super energy-providing grain, so it's difficult to find a reason not to include it in your baby's diet. It also has the added benefit of being a source of iron, protein, fibre, and minerals. Combine it with diced chicken, a confetti of colourful veggies, and a tasty dressing for a yummy meal. The bulgur wheat can be replaced with quinoa if necessary.

BULGUR WHEAT SALAD WITH CHICKEN

❄ **Not suitable for freezing**

Makes 4 portions • Suitable from 24 weeks • Prep time 8 minutes • Cooking time 15 minutes • Provides energy, protein, vitamin A, fibre • Dairy-free

75g (2½oz) bulgur wheat or quinoa

3 tbsp tinned sweetcorn, drained

75g (2½oz) cooked chicken, diced

½ carrot, peeled and grated

6 cherry tomatoes, quartered

60g (2oz) cooked peas

Dressing

1½ tbsp rice wine vinegar

1½ tbsp apple juice

3 tbsp olive oil

1 Put the bulgur wheat, or quinoa, into a pan with 125ml (4½fl oz) water. Cover and bring to the boil.

2 Boil for 1 minute, then set aside off the heat for 15 minutes, until soft and all the water has been absorbed. Leave to cool. If using quinoa, place in a pan of boiling water and simmer for about 25 minutes – follow the instructions on the packet.

3 Place the cooled bulgur wheat in a bowl and then add and mix together the remaining ingredients.

4 Combine the dressing ingredients together and pour over the salad.

5 Refrigerate the remaining portions for up to 2 days.

Flex it...

Replace the chicken with a cooked tasty salmon fillet to give your baby a boost of omega-3 (see page 16).

Instead of peas add half a chopped red pepper, which contains the highest amount of vitamin C of any pepper.

EXPLORING NEW TASTES AND TEXTURES // Stage Two – 6 to 9 months

Beef is a good source of easily absorbed iron, which your baby needs for healthy growth, development, and optimum energy levels.

BEGINNER'S BEEF CASSEROLE

❄ **Suitable for freezing**

Makes 5 portions • Suitable from 6 months • Prep time 10 minutes • Cooking time 1 hour 10 minutes • Provides energy, protein, fibre, iron, vitamin A, zinc • Dairy-free

1 tbsp olive oil

1 small onion, peeled and chopped

1 garlic clove, peeled and crushed

115g (4oz) lean stewing steak, trimmed of fat and cut into small cubes

1 large carrot, peeled and diced

1 large potato, peeled and diced

3 dried apricots, chopped

150ml (5fl oz) passata (sieved tomatoes)

200–250ml (7–8fl oz) unsalted chicken or vegetable stock or water

1 Heat the oil in a small flameproof casserole or heavy-based saucepan and sauté the onion gently for 3 minutes, stirring.

2 Add the garlic and sauté for 30 seconds. Add the stewing steak and sauté, stirring, until browned all over.

3 Add the carrot, potato, and dried apricots, and pour over the passata and stock or water. Bring to the boil, stir well, reduce the heat as low as possible, cover, and simmer gently for about 1 hour, until the meat is tender, adding a little more stock or water if necessary and stirring occasionally.

4 Cool slightly, then purée in a food processor, or place in a bowl and use a hand-blender. For older babies chop by hand to the desired consistency.

5 Freeze in individual portions. When needed, thaw overnight in the fridge or for 1–2 hours at room temperature, then reheat until piping hot. Stir and allow to cool before serving.

For baby-led weaning, cut a small piece of steak into strips. Marinate in 1 tablespoon of olive oil, half a teaspoon of chopped thyme, and half a clove of garlic, bashed, for 10–15 minutes. Remove from the marinade and fry for about 2 minutes each side until cooked.

Beginner's Beef Casserole

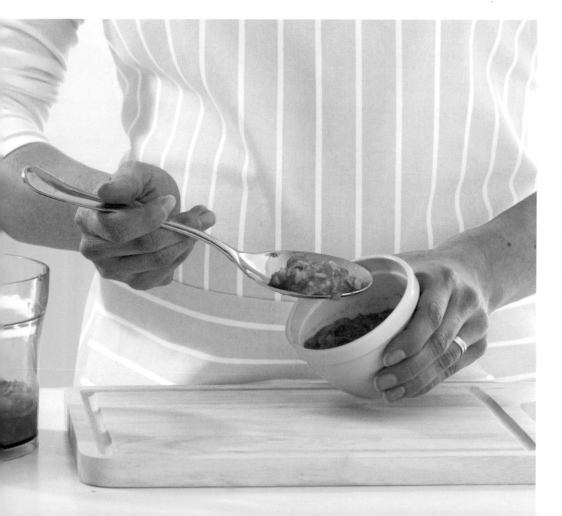

Red meat is your baby's best source of iron and she will love it cooked with apple and sweet-tasting root vegetables, such as sweet potato or parsnip. Some babies reject meat because of its texture; however, the sweet potato and apple in this recipe give the meat a nice smooth texture — not to mention a slightly sweet flavour that babies love.

BEEF CASSEROLE WITH SWEET POTATO

❄ **Suitable for freezing**

Makes 4 portions • Suitable from 6 months • Prep time 12 minutes • Cooking time 1 hour 25 minutes • Provides energy, protein, fibre, iron, vitamin A, zinc • Dairy-free

1 tbsp olive oil

1 small red onion, peeled and chopped

½ celery stick, strings removed and chopped

1 medium carrot, peeled and diced

1 garlic clove, peeled and crushed

115g (4oz) lean stewing steak, trimmed of fat and cut into small cubes

1 tbsp tomato purée

1 small sweet potato (about 250g/9oz), peeled and diced

1 small eating apple, peeled and chopped

1½ tsp chopped fresh thyme or ½ tsp dried thyme

250ml (8fl oz) unsalted chicken or vegetable stock or water

2 tbsp apple juice

1 Preheat the oven to 160°C (fan 140°C), gas 3.

2 Heat the oil in a casserole and sauté the onion, celery, and carrot for 5 minutes, stirring until softened and lightly browned. Add the garlic and sauté for 1 minute, stirring.

3 Stir in the cubes of meat and sauté for 2–3 minutes until browned. Stir in the remaining ingredients. Bring to the boil then cover and cook in the oven for 1 hour. Stir halfway through. After 1 hour, remove the lid and continue to cook for another 15 minutes.

4 Purée until smooth in a food processor or place in a bowl and use a hand-blender. For older babies, chop in a food processor or by hand to the desired consistency.

5 Freeze in individual portions. When needed, thaw overnight in the fridge or for 1–2 hours at room temperature, then microwave or reheat in a small pan until piping hot. Stir and allow to cool before serving.

This fresh fruity dessert is a lovely after-dinner treat for little ones, or you can stir it into a little porridge for breakfast. With a good boost of vitamin C and antioxidants, it's a nutritious treat and a perfect start to the day.

APPLE AND BLACKBERRY COMPÔTE

❄ **Suitable for freezing**

Makes 3–4 portions • Suitable from 6 months • Prep time 5 minutes • Cooking time 20 minutes • Provides fibre • Dairy-free

2 sweet eating apples, peeled, cored, and diced

200ml (7fl oz) apple juice

150g (5¹/₂oz) ripe blackberries

¹/₂ tsp natural vanilla extract

1 tbsp agave syrup or maple syrup (optional)

1 Put the diced apples in a heavy-based saucepan with the apple juice. Bring to the boil, cover, reduce the heat, and cook for 8–10 minutes until the apples are soft. Uncover and simmer until the liquid evaporates, stirring occasionally.

2 Stir in the blackberries and cook for 3–4 minutes until the berries are soft.

3 For young babies, puree the mixture in a food processor or place in a bowl and use a hand-blender, then pass through a sieve to remove the seeds. Stir in the vanilla and syrup, if using. For older babies, simply mash the fruit together.

4 Freeze in individual portions. When needed, thaw overnight in the fridge or for 1–2 hours at room temperature.

To boost the calcium content, make a creamy apple and blackberry fool, by combining 2–3 tablespoons of Apple and Blackberry Compôte with 2 tablespoons of thick full-fat vanilla yogurt. Chill until ready to serve.

Flex it...

Replace the blackberries with blueberries – you won't need to sieve out any seeds.

Apple and Blackberry Compôte

The sweet taste and velvety texture of this smooth purée will make it a firm favourite with even the faddiest of eaters.

APPLE AND PEAR WITH APRICOTS

Suitable for freezing

Makes 4 portions • Suitable from 6 months • Prep time 8 minutes • Cooking time 8 minutes
• Provides fibre, iron, potassium • Dairy-free

2 sweet eating apples, peeled, cored, and diced

2 ripe pears, peeled, cored, and diced

8 dried apricots, cut into small pieces

75ml (5 tbsp) water or apple juice

1 Put the fruit into a heavy-based saucepan with the water or apple juice. Bring to the boil, reduce the heat, cover, and cook gently for about 8 minutes until tender, adding a little more water or juice if necessary.

2 Blend the fruit to the desired consistency in a food processor or place in a bowl and use a hand-blender.

3 Freeze in individual portions. When needed, thaw overnight in the fridge or for 1–2 hours at room temperature.

Plum and blueberry skins provide plenty of healthy fibre; however, if your baby prefers a very smooth purée, you can sieve these out before serving.

APPLE AND PLUM WITH BLUEBERRIES

Suitable for freezing

Makes 3 portions • Suitable from 6 months • Prep time 8 minutes • Cooking time 8 minutes
• Provides fibre, iron, potassium, vitamin K • Dairy-free

2 sweet eating apples, peeled, cored, and diced

2 ripe plums, skinned (see tip, page 95), stoned, and diced

55g (2oz) blueberries

50ml (3 tbsp) water or pure apple juice (not concentrate)

1 Put the apples, plums, and blueberries in a saucepan with the water or juice. Heat until bubbling, cover, reduce the heat, and simmer for about 8 minutes until really tender, adding a spoonful more water or juice, if necessary.

2 Blend the fruit to the desired consistency in a food processor or place in a bowl and use a hand-blender.

3 Freeze in individual portions. When needed, thaw overnight in the fridge or for 1–2 hours at room temperature.

Velvety apricots. The combination of apricots with apple and pear creates a whole new texture for your baby to experience.

The autumnal flavours of this delicious purée are ideal on their own, and also blend well with full-fat yogurt or a little baby rice. Choose plums of any colour and size; in fact, the greater the variety, the higher the nutrient value of the purée. If you choose to include the cinnamon, it will add a warm, rich flavour.

PEAR AND PLUM COMPÔTE

Suitable for freezing

Makes 3 portions • Suitable from 6 months • Prep time 8 minutes • Cooking time 20–30 minutes • Provides vitamin K, fibre • Dairy-free

100ml (3½fl oz) concentrated pure apple juice

2 ripe pears, peeled, cored, and diced

3 large plums, skinned (see tip, page 95), pitted, and chopped

Small pinch ground cinnamon (optional)

Few drops natural vanilla extract

1 Boil the apple juice for 3–5 minutes until reduced by half.

2 Put the pears, plums, and cinnamon in a heavy-based saucepan. Cover and cook gently for 5–10 minutes, until the juices run from the fruit.

3 Uncover and simmer for 10–20 minutes, until the fruit is soft and the liquid has evaporated (the cooking time will depend on the ripeness of the fruit). Stir in the concentrated pure apple juice and the vanilla extract.

4 Mash or purée in a food processor, place in a bowl and use a hand-blender, or pass through a sieve.

5 Freeze in individual portions. When required, thaw overnight in the fridge or for 1–2 hours at room temperature before serving.

This planner is for when you have been able to progress to three meals a day. It's important that meals are made up of two courses to provide all the critical nutrients (see pages 14–17). In addition to the milk feeds shown, your baby may need a mid-morning and a night-time feed.

MENU PLANNER: 6/7 TO 9 MONTHS

DAY	BREAKFAST	LUNCH	MID-AFTERNOON	TEA	BEDTIME
1	Purple Porridge (p.86) with dates/stick of cheese/fruit	Sweet Potato and Kale Croquettes (p.90)/yogurt	Breast/bottle	Beginner's Beef Casserole (p.114)/fruit	Breast/bottle
2	Scrambled egg/ fingers of toast/ fruit	Poached Salmon with Carrots and Peas (p.99)/fruit/ yogurt	Breast/bottle	Tomato and Butternut Squash Pasta (p.96); yogurt	Breast/bottle
3	Toast fingers with cream cheese or peanut butter/ fruit	Chicken and Apple Balls (p.111); broccoli/yogurt	Breast/bottle	Lentil Purée with Sweet Potato (p.95)/ Pear and Plum Compote (p.120)	Breast/bottle
4	Iron-fortified cereal/fruit	Beef Casserole with Sweet Potato (p.116)/yogurt	Breast/bottle	Potato, Carrot, and Sweetcorn (p.88)/fruit	Breast/bottle
5	Iron-fortified cereal/fruit	Annabel's Tasty Salmon (p.104)/ fruit/yogurt	Breast/bottle	Mild Chicken and Apricot Curry (p.106)/ yogurt	Breast/bottle
6	Omelette or scrambled egg with wholegrain toast/fruit	Beginner's Beef Casserole (p.114)/ carrots/apple and plum with blueberries	Breast/bottle	Cod with Butternut Squash (p.100)/ fruit	Breast/bottle
7	Iron-fortified cereal/yogurt/ fruit	Bulgur Wheat Salad with Chicken (p.112)/fruit/yogurt	Breast/bottle	Sweet Potato with Broccoli and Peas (p.87)/yogurt	Breast/bottle

Creating a varied diet

Stage Three – 9 to 12 months

Once your baby is **happy with a variety** of foods and textures, he'll become used to the idea of mealtimes and work towards **eating three meals a day.** As his milk intake decreases, it becomes increasingly important that **his diet is balanced.** You can adjust family meals to make them appropriate for his little tummy, and encourage him to eat along **with the whole family.**

• *Menu planner page 156*

A BALANCED DIET

As your baby heads towards his first birthday, and you begin to give him fewer milk feeds, it becomes even more important that his diet is balanced and varied. His tummy is small, so everything he eats should contribute something to his overall nutritional intake.

How to plan your baby's diet

A balanced diet includes a variety of different foods. We know that babies need critical nutrients (see pages 14–17), and these are best provided through a varied diet. Offer a range of proteins such as pulses, fish, chicken, eggs, and yogurt. Wheat-based pastas or breads are a good source of carbohydrates, but include rice, potatoes, and different grains, too.

Experiment with fruit and vegetables, offering sweet potatoes and butternut squash in place of traditional favourites, and berries and exotic fruits, such as mango, instead of apples and bananas. Go for spring greens, spinach, or kale, and peppers and courgettes for colour and key nutrients. The wider the range, the better.

Creating a balance

Including food from the four food groups helps to meet your baby's nutritional requirements:
- Potatoes, bread, rice, pasta, and other starchy carbohydrates
- Fruit and vegetables
- Beans, pulses, fish, eggs, meat; other proteins
- Dairy and alternatives.

Babies and toddlers eat smaller amounts of food than older children and adults, so it's important for them to eat regular meals and nutritious snacks. Babies need fat in their diet, so make sure that your little one is getting enough healthy fats (EFAs) (see page 16).

Five a day. Lightly steamed vegetables as a finger food snack help make sure your baby gets his five a day.

Three meals a day

At this stage your baby will be eating three meals and three snacks per day, although the amount actually eaten will vary. It's not unusual for one meal to be received better than the others, or perhaps your baby is a grazer, and that's fine, too. Don't forget, the purpose of weaning is to move away from milk and

Which food will your baby try today?

Aim for a good intake of critical nutrients.

towards food. Although your baby needs around 500–600ml (16fl oz–1 pint) of milk per day, it can be helpful for you to decide when you want him to have it rather than feeding on demand.

In the morning give him a little less milk so that he's more likely to eat a good breakfast, or if your baby is a late riser skip the early morning feed and give him milk at breakfast. You may choose to give him the rest of his milk feeds in between meals with a snack, or if it's easier give milk as a drink with meals instead of water, but don't offer this until he's at least halfway through his food, so that he doesn't fill up on milk.

Your baby will know when he is full. The professional advice now is not to encourage "one more spoonful" as this confuses a baby's in-built mechanism to self-regulate his appetite.

What can I offer for dessert?

By around 10 months, your baby's meals should consist of two courses – a main course and dessert or a starter and a main. This may sound

Time for pudding. Yogurt mixed with fruit purée, such as peach, is a healthier choice than ready-flavoured yogurt.

decadent, but there is a scientific reason for it. An extra course offers your baby a new taste and texture and another opportunity to get those critical nutrients. Good pudding ideas are fresh fruit, a home-made cookie (see page 152), fresh-fruit ice lolly (see page 154), yogurt, or cheese cubes and breadsticks!

HEALTHY SNACKS

Snacks are another way of ensuring your baby gets adequate amounts of critical nutrients. At this stage, he should be having three small but nutritious snacks per day in between meals. Try to make sure that snacks contain at least two food items that contain the critical nutrients, one of which could be his milk. For example:

- Buttered fruit toast/hot cross bun
- Peanut butter on toast
- Pitta and hummus
- Fruit and a yogurt
- Chunks of cheese and breadsticks
- Rice cakes and milk
- Mini tuna sandwiches (see page 133)

MOVING ON TO NEW TEXTURES

Not all babies take kindly to lumps in their food, but most will master a variety of textures if you persevere. While it's perfectly fine to continue to purée some foods for your baby, by 9 to 12 months the time has come for her to learn to chew and swallow. The good news is that there's lots you can do to encourage her to enjoy expanding her food repertoire!

Mashing, mincing, and chopping

Mashing vegetables together, such as potato, carrot, and broccoli with a little butter, milk, and grated cheese, is a good way to introduce different textures. You can also mash well-cooked and raw fruit, and it's a good way to blend several fruits and/or vegetables together without the use of your food processor. Mincing foods will also produce pieces that are whole enough to have a little bite, but soft enough to be chewed and swallowed easily. Once minced and mashed foods are accepted by your little one, try finely cutting and chopping her food, gradually increasing the size of the pieces as she becomes accustomed to the new texture. Some babies actually prefer larger, identifiable lumps to smaller ones that take them by surprise.

> " *While it's perfectly fine to continue to purée some foods for your baby, the time has come for her to learn to chew and swallow.* "

Meat, poultry, and other proteins

Meat can sometimes be difficult for babies to chew, and this can put them off, so mixing cooked minced meat or chicken with pasta or mashed potato is good, or you can make mini meat or chicken balls or mini burgers. Pieces of roast chicken make good finger food. Alternatively, you can serve up breaded chicken or fish fingers. Tougher cuts of meat such as lamb and beef can be slow-cooked to make them more tender and easier to manage. You could also consider adding tiny pieces of meat to pastas and risottos, where they aren't quite so overwhelming.

Try offering healthy proteins, such as pulses, whole, in the form of finger foods. For example, chickpeas, butter beans, and even kidney beans are usually happily eaten by babies when you serve them this way.

Mixing textures

Create a little plate for your baby that offers foods of all sorts of textures. For example, you could cook some minced chicken balls, mash some potatoes, and offer some raw vegetables, such as carrot or cucumber, with a tasty dip. Or whizz together some cooked vegetables, such as carrots, courgettes, and sweet pepper, with a tomato sauce, and serve with pasta shapes, followed by a home-made cookie or mini muffin. You can also offer a variety of fruit, vegetables, meat, fish or poultry, dairy, and carbs at the same meal, allowing her to choose some from a tray of finger foods, and feeding her some

Mash, mince, grate, or chop!

Let your baby explore the textures with her hands.

of the smoother foods from a spoon. She'll end up chewing the finger foods at the same time as she takes in whatever you are offering on the spoon, blending the different flavours and textures. Encourage her to use her finger foods to dip and mush other foods on her plate. She'll be able to create her own concoctions, which will have a texture all of their own. It's good to have a plate or bowl with divisions, as babies like to keep different foods separate.

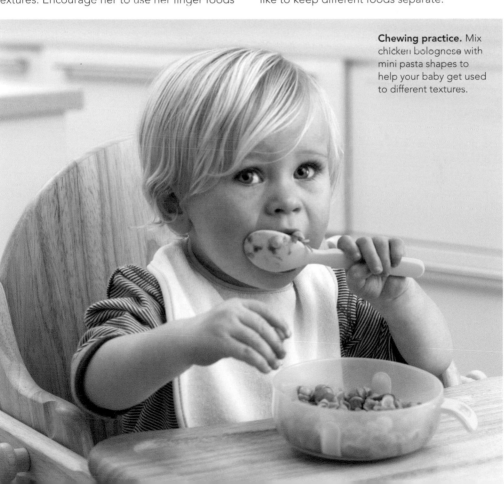

Chewing practice. Mix chicken bolognese with mini pasta shapes to help your baby get used to different textures.

Moving on to New Textures

SUCCESSFUL SELF-FEEDING

All babies will eventually learn to feed themselves and if you opted for baby-led weaning, your baby will have had plenty of practice already. You can encourage self-feeding by allowing your baby to experiment. Let him play with his food and make sure you give him plenty of finger foods to suck, gnaw, or actually eat, alongside every meal.

How long does it take?

Most little ones are unable to feed themselves properly using cutlery before they are at least two or three years old, and until that time, they will rely on mum, dad, or their carer to make sure that the right amount of food makes it into their mouths. Your baby may object to you feeding him if he is feeling particularly independent, and you may have a tussle on your hands as you try to take charge again. You can, however, usually distract him in order to get a little food into his mouth, or help him guide his spoon in the right direction. Try to feed him a good proportion of his meal, so that you know exactly what he's getting. Although some babies can clear a bowl themselves in record time, chances are that most of its contents will end up in their bib, down the sides of their highchair, or scattered all over the floor.

Give your baby a small spoon or soft, flexible fork with a chubby handle that he can grip easily and allow him to scoop the contents of his bowl (or yours!) towards his mouth. Encourage him to pick up finger foods, too. Most things end up in a baby's mouth at this age, so it's a good habit to encourage, as he'll be more likely to try new things if he feels he's in the driving seat.

He'll probably use his hands to eat even the messiest foods for many months to come, so be prepared by using bibs and putting a splash

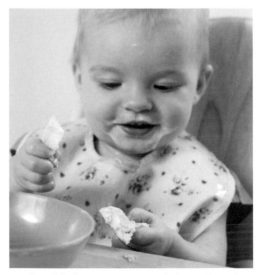

Touch and feel. Encouraging your baby to play with food is a key part of the weaning process, as she learns how to eat.

mat under the high chair so that food that is dropped on the floor can be recycled or more easily cleared up.

Playing with food

This is an important part of the developmental process of learning to eat, so it should be encouraged. The mess may be dispiriting, but your baby should be allowed to touch and feel his food, and to guide it in the direction of his mouth without fear of upsetting you.

He'll discover the way the different textures feel and taste, and will be interested in discovering new wonders.

Reluctant self-feeders

Some babies are simply not interested in feeding themselves and rely on you entirely to get food from bowl to mouth. While your baby is still very much dependent at this age and does require regular feeding alongside any self-feeding efforts, it is a good idea to encourage him to try. Why not buy a bright new set of cutlery for him and give him a bowl that's all his own? Present it with a flourish and show him what to do. It's important to remember that babies are not born knowing how to use a spoon or fork, so you can guide his hand at every meal, or show him by doing it yourself, until he gets the hang of it.

> " *Let him play with his food and give him plenty of finger foods to suck, gnaw, or actually eat, alongside every meal.* "

You may want to give him a bowl of food at the outset of his meal, when he's more hungry, and leave him to it for five minutes or so. Chances are he'll manage to get at least something into his mouth. Furthermore, babies are great mimics and like nothing better than being like mum and dad, or siblings. Give your baby plenty of opportunity to share mealtimes with the whole family, and he'll soon work out what he's supposed to be doing.

If all the above fail, don't panic. Your baby may just enjoy the process of being fed and will get to grips with the basics later on. Continue to inspire him with delicious meals, and praise his efforts.

DAVID ASKS . . .

My baby flings his bowl across the room and throws everything on his tray. I have no idea how much he's eating and the mess is driving me crazy!

First of all, you will need to accept that most babies are messy, and eating with their hands, playing with food, and mushing it between their fingers all encourage them to learn about different foods. In my experience, babies who are allowed to play with their food tend to be better eaters, because they enjoy mealtimes, have the opportunity to experiment, and learn to self-feed that much earlier.

Having said that, you can set a few basic ground rules. You can discourage him from throwing food by expressing your disapproval, and taking away his bowl each time he does this. You can also dispense with the bowl for the time being, placing his food directly on his tray, or investing in a bowl with a suction cup at the base to prevent it from being lifted.

You may also want to consider whether he's bored. Maybe he's had enough and wants to get out. Try removing the high chair tray and pulling him up to the table to eat with the rest of the family.

FAMILY FOOD

One of the best parts of introducing your baby to a greater variety of tastes and textures is that she can become involved in family meals. Some recipes must be adjusted to make sure your baby isn't having too much sugar or salt, but this can make the whole family more aware of what's in their food.

Adapting family meals

Most whole, fresh foods are appropriate for babies and you'll simply need to be sure that you don't add salt or sugar (watch the condiments and cooking sauces, too). So, roasting a chicken, mashing some potatoes, and serving up some creamed spinach and baby carrots will provide the perfect meal for a little one. Finely chop, mash, or even purée the chicken and carrots and your child's meal is ready without further cooking. Similarly, you can whizz family soups, stews, casseroles, and even pasta dishes in your food processor for a moment or two, perhaps adding a little extra liquid to make it easier for your baby to manage.

> "
> *Sharing mealtimes helps to create healthy, positive associations with food, as your baby learns to enjoy the social experience.*
> "

What about herbs and spices?

Herbs are a delicious and nutritious addition to baby foods and can spice up, or make more fragrant, foods that might otherwise seem a little flavourless. Unlike salt and sugar, there are no specific spices or herbs that need to be off the menu for babies, but some babies simply do not like the taste of some flavourings and others may have their tummies upset by them.

It's a good idea to try one new flavouring at a time and if there appears to be no problem you can move on to try whatever your baby likes. Any of the green herbs, such as coriander, basil, thyme, parsley, and dill, can be added easily, and you can use cinnamon, rosemary, and bay leaves while cooking fish, chicken, or vegetables. The more flavours to which your little one becomes accustomed while she's small, the wider the variety of "likes" that will be established.

If your baby likes the flavours and has no reactions after eating them (watch for diarrhoea, crying, rashes, and drawn-up knees), then you can introduce whatever spices appeal. In some cultures, babies are brought up on strong, spicy foods and cope very well. So experiment to see what your baby will enjoy.

The importance of eating together

Sharing mealtimes helps to create healthy, positive associations with food, as your baby learns to enjoy the social experience. Studies show that children who eat with their parents are more likely to consume more fruits and vegetables and eat fewer fatty and sugary foods. The reason is that they develop good habits based on the family ethos and also eat a wider range of foods, which they will try because everyone is eating them. Most babies love to copy parents and siblings, so offer your baby a little of your food and you'll be amazed by what she will eat.

OUT AND ABOUT

While it's a good idea to stay at home when you first start the weaning process, the time will quickly arrive when you'll need to feed your baby while you are out and about. You may also need to prepare meals for her to eat at nursery or at the childminder's.

Transporting your baby's food

A good cool bag, with an ice pack, should keep your baby's purées at the right temperature. If you need to keep a purée chilled for a long period of time, you could invest in a wide-necked flask into which you can place some chilled purée or several frozen purée cubes. Make sure you heat the purée until piping hot and then let it cool before serving, to destroy any bacteria.

Many finger foods are easy to transport, and will last a few hours at room temperature. Fruit and vegetables, bread fingers, mini sandwiches, rice cakes, and dried fruits will all keep your baby's tummy full, no matter where you are. You can also choose foods that can be puréed, mashed, or cut into chunks on the spot, such as bananas, mango, papaya, or very ripe pears or peaches.

Your baby's lunchbox

Plan a lunchbox to include foods from the groups below. There should always be:
- Protein, such as meat, fish, eggs, hummus, yogurt, cheese, or beans
- Dairy, such as yogurt, cheese, or milk
- Fruit
- Vegetables or salad
- Carbohydrate, such as bread, crackers, couscous, pasta, or rice
- A drink – water or milk.

Note: it's fine to include a small lunchbox treat, such as a flapjack, brownie, cookie, crisps, popcorn, or pretzels.

A taste of home. When you are heading out for the day, create a delicious lunchbox from your baby's favourite finger foods.

You can add child appeal by threading bite-sized pieces of fruit or veggies onto a straw or cutting sandwiches into shapes.

As your child gets older, involve her in making her own lunchbox healthy treats such as my Banana Muffins (see page 151) or Sultana and Oat Cookies (see page 152).

Eating out

If your baby is keen to try something from your plate, let her! While restaurant foods are likely to be high in salt or sugar, a tiny taste won't do any long-term damage and may encourage a sophisticated palate. Take a suitable weaning meal with you so she can eat alongside you.

Eggs are so nutritious that they are often referred to as nature's multivitamin. As well as this scrambled egg, you can now give your baby runny eggs (see page 74).

EGG, SPINACH, AND TOMATO MUFFIN

❄ **Not suitable for freezing**

Makes 1 portion • Suitable from 9 months • Prep time 5 minutes • Cooking time 5 minutes
• Provides energy, protein, iron, zinc, B vitamins, vitamin K, wide variety of minerals

2 knobs of butter or dairy-free spread

1 spring onion, chopped

20g (¾oz) baby spinach, chopped

3 cherry tomatoes, quartered

1 large egg

1 tbsp whole milk or a suitable dairy-free formula milk for under 12 months or almond milk for over 12 months

½ English muffin or wheat- or gluten-free alternative

1 Melt one knob of butter in a small frying pan. Add the spring onion and fry for 30 seconds. Add the spinach and tomatoes and stir over the heat for 2 minutes until soft. Spoon into a bowl.

2 Add the remaining butter to the pan. Beat the egg and milk together, then pour into the hot pan. Stir, using a wooden spoon, until scrambled. Return the spinach and tomatoes to the pan and gently fold in.

3 Toast the muffin until golden. Once cooled, spoon the egg mixture on top and serve.

Tomato and pasta are a match made in heaven. This delicious and healthy dish is perfect finger food for your baby.

TOMATO AND PESTO BRUSCHETTA

❄ **Not suitable for freezing**

Makes 4 • Suitable from 9 months • Prep time 10 minutes • Cooking time 15 minutes
• Provides energy, fibre • Dairy-free

12 cherry tomatoes, halved

2 spring onions, chopped

½ garlic clove, crushed

1 tsp pesto

3 basil leaves, chopped

4 × thin slices of ciabatta bread or wheat- or gluten-free alternative

1 tbsp olive oil, plus 1 tsp for roasting

1 Preheat the oven to 200°C (fan 180°C), gas 6.

2 Put the tomatoes, spring onions, garlic, pesto, and the teaspoon of oil into a small roasting tin. Mix together. Roast in the preheated oven for 10 minutes until softened, then stir in the chopped basil.

3 Brush one side of the bread with the oil. Place on a small baking sheet and bake for 5 minutes.

4 Arrange the bread on a plate and, once cooled down, spoon the roasted tomatoes over the top.

Sandwiches are quick and easy to prepare and make good finger food. When friends bring their babies round, you can make a variety of different flavours – and offer them to hungry mums and dads as well. For young babies it may be better to cut off the crusts from the bread and then flatten the sandwich with a rolling pin. Wholemeal bread is an easier texture to manage than white bread.

MINI SANDWICHES TO SHARE

Banana, Cream Cheese, and Raspberry

Suitable from 10 months • Provides energy, protein, calcium

2 tsp full-fat cream cheese or dairy-free alternative
2 slices bread or wheat- or gluten-free alternative
½ small banana, mashed
2 tsp raspberry pure fruit spread or low-sugar jam

Spread the cream cheese over one slice of bread and spread the mashed banana over the cream cheese. Spread the jam over the second slice of bread and sandwich the two slices together. Cut into eight small squares.

Tuna or Salmon Mayonnaise

Suitable from 10 months • Provides energy, protein, omega-3 EFAs, vitamin D, vitamin B12 • Dairy-free

2 tbsp drained canned tuna or salmon, flaked
2 tsp mayonnaise
1 tsp tomato ketchup
2 slices bread or wheat- or gluten-free alternative

Mash together the tuna or salmon with the mayonnaise and tomato ketchup. Spread over one slice of bread and sandwich together with the second slice. Cut into eight small squares.

Tip:
Only use commercial mayonnaise made with processed egg, rather than mayonnaise made with raw egg. Alternatively, use a little Greek yogurt instead.

Other good fillings ...

- Grated cheese
- Cream cheese and chopped, dried apricots
- Chopped hard-boiled egg mixed with a little mayonnaise and snipped chives
- Mashed sardines with a little tomato ketchup
- Mashed banana

Stirring in fresh basil and Parmesan is a good way to add flavour as you can't season the delicious creamy tomato sauce used in this recipe with salt. You can freeze the sauce on its own in individual portions then reheat and add to freshly cooked pasta before serving if you prefer.

TOMATO AND BASIL PASTA

❄ **Suitable for freezing**

Makes 4 portions • Suitable from 9 months • Prep time 5 minutes • Cooking time 20 minutes • Provides protein, fibre, calcium, and energy

1 tbsp olive oil

½ small onion, peeled and chopped

½ garlic clove, peeled and crushed

1 small carrot, peeled and grated

200ml (7fl oz) passata (sieved tomatoes)

3 tbsp water

2 fresh basil leaves, roughly chopped

1 tsp Parmesan cheese or dairy-free alternative, grated

1 tbsp full-fat cream cheese or dairy-free alternative

55g (2oz) conchigliette (baby pasta shells) or wheat- or gluten-free alternative

1 Heat the oil in a saucepan. Add the onion, garlic, and carrot, stir, cover, and cook gently for 5 minutes to soften.

2 Add the passata and water. Bring to the boil, reduce the heat, cover, and simmer gently for 15 minutes

3 Purée the sauce with the basil and cheeses in a food processor or place in a bowl and use a hand-blender.

4 Meanwhile, cook the pasta shells in boiling water according to the packet instructions. Drain and return to the pan. Stir in the sauce, cool slightly, and serve.

5 Freeze in individual portions. When needed, thaw overnight in the fridge or for 1–2 hours at room temperature, then microwave or reheat in a small pan until piping hot. Stir and allow to cool before serving.

Flex it...

Try grated celeriac or courgette in place of the grated carrot.

If your baby likes moist textures, mix this with a little Tomato and Basil Pasta (see opposite) or a spoonful of warm passata before serving.

CHERUB'S COUSCOUS

❄ **Suitable for freezing**

Makes 3–4 portions • Suitable from 9 months • Prep time 10 minutes • Cooking time 15 minutes • Provides energy, protein, vitamin C, calcium, fibre

2 tsp olive oil

½ small onion, peeled and chopped

¼ orange pepper, deseeded and chopped

1 small chicken breast, cut into small cubes

½ garlic clove, peeled and crushed

2 tbsp frozen peas

90ml (3fl oz) unsalted chicken or vegetable stock or water

75g (2½oz) quick cooking couscous or wheat- or gluten-free alternative

15g (½oz) Parmesan cheese or dairy-free alternative, grated

1 Heat the oil in a saucepan and sauté the onion, pepper, and chicken gently for 3 minutes, stirring. Stir in the garlic and sauté for 30 seconds.

2 Add the peas and stock or water, bring to the boil, reduce the heat, cover, and simmer gently for 5 minutes, or until the chicken and vegetables are tender.

3 Stir in the couscous, remove from the heat, cover, and leave to stand for 5 minutes. Fluff the couscous with a fork and mix in the Parmesan before serving.

4 Freeze in individual portions. When needed, thaw overnight in the fridge or for 1–2 hours at room temperature, then microwave or reheat in a small pan until piping hot. Stir and allow to cool before serving.

Flex it...

Use a turkey breast instead of chicken.

Use any colour pepper – they are all packed with health-giving nutrients!

Cherub's Couscous

This delicious dish is bursting with flavour and, like most pasta dishes, it is very quick and easy to make.

PASTA "RISOTTO"

❄ **Suitable for freezing**

Makes 4 portions • Suitable from 9 months • Prep time 5 minutes • Cooking time 11 minutes • Provides energy, protein, calcium, zinc, vitamin A

75g (2½oz) orzo or wheat- or gluten-free orzo or other small pasta

1 small carrot, peeled and cut into very small dice

250ml (8fl oz) boiling water

1 small courgette, peeled and cut into very small dice

3 tbsp frozen peas

15g (½oz) unsalted butter, cut into small flakes

30g (1oz) Parmesan cheese or dairy-free alternative, grated

1 Put the pasta in a saucepan together with the carrot. Cover with the boiling water, bring back to the boil, stir, reduce the heat, cover, and simmer gently for 5 minutes.

2 Add the courgette, re-cover, and cook for 3 minutes. Stir in the peas and cook for a further 3 minutes.

3 Stir in the butter and Parmesan. Cool slightly before serving.

4 Freeze in individual portions. When needed, thaw overnight in the fridge or for 1–2 hours at room temperature, then microwave or reheat in a small pan until piping hot. Stir and allow to cool before serving.

You could serve these with Mini Meatballs (see page 150) or Annabel's Chicken Burgers (see page 144) or with carrot, cucumber, or sweet pepper sticks. They are also good served with the Tomato and Basil Pasta (see page 134) as a dipping sauce.

CHEESY RICE BALLS

❄ **Suitable for freezing**

Makes 22 balls, 5–6 portions • Suitable from 9 months • Prep time 5 minutes • Cooking time 20 minutes • Provides energy, protein, zinc, calcium, B vitamins

100g (3½oz) risotto rice
250ml (8fl oz) unsalted vegetable stock or water
55g (2oz) Cheddar cheese or dairy-free alternative, grated
15g (½oz) Parmesan cheese or dairy-free alternative, grated
2 tsp finely chopped chives
Pepper, to taste

1 Put the rice and stock or water in a small non-stick saucepan and bring to the boil. Reduce the heat as low as possible, cover, and simmer gently for 10 minutes.

2 Add 2 tablespoons water, stir, re-cover, and cook for a further 10 minutes, until the stock has been absorbed and the rice is tender.

3 Remove from the heat and leave to stand for 5 minutes, then transfer to a bowl and leave for 10–15 minutes until cool enough to handle. Stir in the cheese and chives, and season with pepper to taste.

4 Roll teaspoonfuls into balls using your hands. Serve straight away or place in a sealed container and chill immediately. The balls will keep in the fridge for 24 hours or can be frozen then thawed overnight in the fridge, not at room temperature.

Flex it...

Replace the chopped chives with the same amount of immunity-boosting chopped parsley.

Cheesy Rice Balls

These individual fish pies are just the right size for your little one and perfect for freezing. Mixing carrot into the topping helps boost your child's five-a-day because potatoes don't count, but carrots do!

MINI FISH PIES

❄ **Suitable for freezing**

Makes 6 portions • Suitable from 9 months • Prep time 15 minutes • Cooking time 20–25 minutes • Provides energy, protein, omega-3 EFAs, vitamin A, vitamin B$_{12}$

40g (1¹/₂oz) butter or dairy-free spread

1 onion, chopped

1 tsp white wine vinegar

3 tbsp flour or gluten-free flour or 1 tbsp cornflour

150ml (5fl oz) fish stock

200ml (7fl oz) whole milk or a suitable dairy-free formula milk for under 12 months or almond milk for over 12 months

6 cherry tomatoes, quartered

1 tbsp freshly chopped dill

25g (³/₄oz) Parmesan cheese or dairy-free alternative, grated

450g (1lb) mixed salmon and cod, diced

Potato topping:

500g (1lb 2oz) white potato, peeled and diced

100g (3¹/₂oz) carrot, chopped

A knob of butter or dairy-free spread

1 tbsp whole milk or a suitable dairy-free formula milk for under 12 months or almond milk for over 12 months

30g (1oz) Parmesan cheese or dairy-free alternative, grated

1 Melt the butter in a saucepan. Add the onion and fry for 5 minutes, then add the vinegar and stir until evaporated. Add the flour. If using cornflour, see step 2.

2 Add the fish stock and milk, bring up to the boil and whisk until thickened. If using cornflour, mix it with 2 tablespoons of cold water and then add to the milk, and stir until thickened.

3 Add the tomatoes, dill, and Parmesan. Stir, then add the fish. Spoon into six ramekins about 10cm (4in) diameter.

4 Preheat the oven to 200°C (fan 180°C), gas 6.

5 Cook the potatoes and carrot in a pan of boiling water until soft. Drain and mash with the butter, milk, and cheese. Spread on top of the pies.

6 Bake in the preheated oven for 20–25 minutes until bubbling. Allow to cool down before serving.

7 Defrost overnight in the fridge or for several hours at room temperature. Reheat in an oven preheated to 180°C (fan 160°C), gas 4 for 15 minutes.

Flex it...

Replace the cod with the same quantity of pollock.

In the potato topping, replace the carrot with swede, a nutritious vegetable that is high in vitamins A and C.

These delicious, golden fish fingers can be served to the whole family, and provide plenty of good-quality protein. If you choose white-skinned fillets, there is no need to remove the skin. However, darker-skinned fillets should have their tougher skins removed before preparing.

FISH FINGERS

❄ **Suitable for freezing, uncooked**

Makes 6–8 fingers, 3–4 portions • Suitable from 9 months • Prep time 10 minutes
• Cooking time 4–6 minutes • Provides energy, protein, calcium, variety of minerals, B vitamins

75g (2¹/₂oz) fresh white breadcrumbs (3 medium slices bread) or wheat- or gluten-free breadcrumbs

20g (³/₄oz) Parmesan cheese or dairy-free alternative, freshly grated

2 tbsp roughly chopped parsley

Good pinch of paprika (optional)

2 fresh (not frozen) flat white boneless fish fillets (eg sole, plaice), about 100g (3¹/₂oz) each, skinned (see above)

2 tbsp plain flour or gluten-free flour

1 egg beaten with 1 tbsp water, or an egg replacement (see page 20)

Vegetable oil for frying

1 Put the breadcrumbs, Parmesan, parsley, and paprika (if using) in a food processor and whizz together until the parsley is finely chopped. Transfer to a large plate.

2 Cut the fish fillets in halves lengthways then into strips the size of little fingers.

3 Put the flour on a plate, and put the beaten egg and water in a shallow dish. Toss each piece of fish in the flour to dust, then dip in the egg, then roll in the breadcrumbs to coat.

4 If you are not cooking straight away, put the coated fish on a baking sheet lined with cling film, cover with a second sheet of cling film and freeze for 2–3 hours until solid. When frozen transfer to a rigid container or sealed plastic bag and store in the freezer.

5 To cook, heat a thin layer of oil in a frying pan. Cook fresh or from frozen for about 2–3 minutes each side, until golden and cooked through. Drain on kitchen paper before serving.

Crushed corn flakes make a delicious coating for fish. Here I have mixed them with cooked quinoa – you could also mix in some grated Parmesan cheese. Instead of baking, fry the fish fingers in sunflower oil if you prefer.

CHUNKY QUINOA FISH FINGERS

❄ **Not suitable for freezing**

Makes 12 • Suitable from 9 months • Prep time 15 minutes • Cooking time 10–12 minutes

• Provides energy, protein, iron, a variety of minerals, several B vitamins

100g (3¹/₂oz) cooked quinoa, cooled

30g (1oz) corn flakes, crushed

1 tbsp freshly chopped parsley

250g (9oz) cod loin fillets, skinned

2 tbsp plain flour or gluten-free flour

1 egg, beaten with 1 tbsp water, or egg replacement (see page 20)

Sunflower oil

Salt (for over 12 months) and freshly ground black pepper

Herb dip:

150g (5¹/₂oz) natural yogurt or dairy-free alternative

2 tbsp mayonnaise

1 tbsp finely chopped fresh parsley

1 tbsp finely chopped fresh chives

1 Preheat the oven to 220°C (fan 200°C), gas 7. Line a baking sheet with non-stick paper.

2 To make the crispy coating, mix the quinoa, corn flakes, and parsley together on a plate.

3 Slice the cod into 12 even-sized fingers. Sprinkle over the flour and season lightly. Dip each fish finger into the beaten egg, then coat in the crumb mixture.

4 Arrange on the baking sheet. Drizzle over a little sunflower oil.

5 Bake in the preheated oven for 10–12 minutes, until lightly golden and crisp. Drain on kitchen paper.

6 Meanwhile, mix the yogurt, mayonnaise, herbs, and seasoning, if using, together in a bowl.

7 Once cooled down, arrange the fish fingers on a plate with the dip.

Flex it...

For an alternative coating, replace the quinoa and corn flakes with 50g (1¾oz) rice krispies and 3 heaped tablespoons Parmesan cheese.

Chunky Quinoa Fish Fingers

This colourful dish will certainly catch your baby's eye. The nutritious red pepper is diced and mixed with rice, chicken, tomatoes, and tasty fresh herbs.

TASTY CHICKEN AND VEGGIE RICE

❄ **Suitable for freezing**

Makes 4–6 portions • Suitable from 9 months • Prep time 15 minutes • Cooking time 20 minutes • Provides energy, protein, fibre, iron, B vitamins • Dairy-free

1 tbsp olive oil
1 red onion, chopped
40g (1¹/₂oz) red pepper, deseeded and diced
1 garlic clove, crushed
400g can chopped tomatoes
4 tbsp apple juice
1 tbsp freshly chopped thyme
1 tbsp sundried tomato paste
120g (4¹/₂oz) cooked chicken, diced
3 tbsp tinned sweetcorn, drained
150g (5¹/₂oz) cooked brown rice
1 tbsp freshly chopped basil

1 Heat the oil in a saucepan. Add the onion and pepper and fry for 5 minutes. Add the garlic and fry for 30 seconds.

2 Add the tomatoes, apple juice, thyme, and tomato paste. Bring to the boil. Cover with a lid and simmer for 10 minutes.

3 Add the chicken, sweetcorn, rice, and basil and stir over the heat for 1 minute, until the chicken is warmed through. Leave to cool before serving.

4 Defrost overnight in the fridge, or for several hours at room temperature. Reheat in an oven preheated to 180°C (fan 160°C), gas 4 for 12 minutes.

For baby-led weaning, see the recipe on the opposite page and the recipe on page 144.

Flex it...

Use cooked chicken thigh meat to boost the consumption of iron.

Replace the brown rice with bulgur wheat.

This yummy mixture of diced chicken, tomatoes, and melted cheese sandwiched between tortillas will be hard for your little one to resist and is a great dish for self-feeding. The Gruyère can be replaced with grated Cheddar if necessary.

CHICKEN QUESADILLA

⚙ **Not suitable for freezing**

Makes 1–2 portions • Suitable from 9 months • Prep time 5 minutes • Cooking time 5 minutes
• Provides energy, protein, calcium, vitamin E, fibre

20g (³⁄₄oz) cooked chicken, finely diced

1 tsp sundried tomato paste

2 cherry tomatoes, chopped

15g (¹⁄₂oz) Gruyère cheese, grated, or dairy-free alternative

1 tbsp tinned sweetcorn, drained

2 mini wraps or mini corn tortillas

1 tsp olive oil

1 Mix the chicken, tomato paste, tomatoes, cheese, and sweetcorn together in a small bowl.

2 Put one wrap onto a board. Spread over the filling. Top with the second wrap.

3 Heat the oil in a small frying pan. Put the quesadilla into the pan. Fry for 1¹⁄₂–2 minutes until golden, then flip over and cook for another 1–2 minutes until golden.

4 Remove from the pan and slice into six wedges, once cooled down.

Chicken Quesadilla

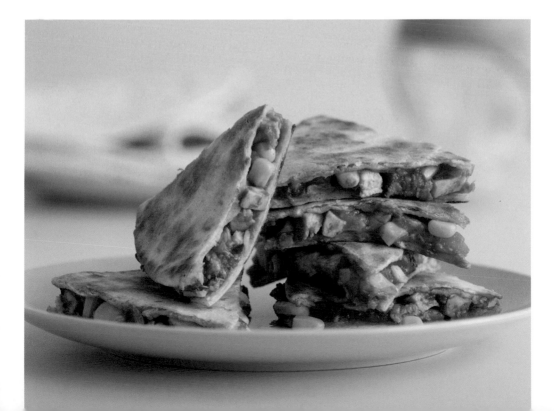

These soft, tasty burgers are bound to be a hit with your child – serve with steamed vegetables, such as carrots or broccoli, for a perfect balanced meal.

ANNABEL'S CHICKEN BURGERS

❄ Suitable for freezing
Makes 12 mini burgers, 4 portions • Suitable from 9 months • Prep time 10 minutes
• Cooking time 10 minutes • Provides protein, iron, zinc, calcium, B vitamins

1 tbsp olive oil
½ small onion, peeled and finely chopped
1 small garlic clove, peeled and crushed
225g (8oz) minced chicken (mix of breast and thigh meat)
4 fresh sage leaves, chopped
½ eating apple, peeled and grated
20g (¾oz) fresh breadcrumbs (1 medium slice bread) or wheat- or gluten-free breadcrumbs
20g (¾oz) Parmesan cheese or dairy-free alternative, grated
Vegetable oil, for frying

1 Heat the olive oil in a small pan and sauté the onion and garlic gently, stirring, for 2 minutes. Allow to cool.

2 In a bowl mix the chicken with the sage, apple, and breadcrumbs. Stir in the onion and garlic and the Parmesan.

3 Using your hands, shape the mixture into 12 small patties.

4 Heat a little vegetable oil in a frying pan and brown the burgers for 1–2 minutes each side. Turn down the heat to low and cook gently for about 5 minutes until cooked through. To test, push the point of a knife down through the centre of one of the burgers. Hold for 5 seconds and remove. The blade should feel burning hot. If not, cook a little longer. Drain on kitchen paper.

5 To freeze, place the burgers (before or after cooking) on a baking sheet lined with cling film, cover with a second sheet of cling film, and freeze for 2–3 hours until solid. Pack in a rigid container or a sealed plastic bag. Defrost overnight in the fridge or for 2–3 hours at room temperature.

CREATING A VARIED DIET // Stage Three – 9 to 12 months

This flavourful dish is a delicious alternative to traditional Bolognese sauce and it works well with any type of pasta. Rich in protein, iron, and antioxidants, it is a balanced meal in a bowl. You can freeze the sauce on its own in individual portions then reheat and serve with freshly cooked pasta if you prefer.

CHICKEN BOLOGNESE

❄ **Suitable for freezing**

Makes 4 portions • Suitable from 9 months • Prep time 10 minutes • Cooking time 15 minutes
• Provides protein, iron, zinc, calcium, fibre, vitamin A • Dairy-free

1 tbsp olive oil
½ small onion, peeled and finely chopped
1 small carrot, peeled and grated
½ large or 1 small garlic clove, peeled and crushed
85g (3oz) minced chicken (I use thigh meat)
½ tsp chopped fresh thyme or good pinch dried thyme
200ml (7fl oz) passata (sieved tomatoes)
100ml (3½fl oz) pure apple juice
1 tsp tomato purée
½ tsp Worcestershire sauce
4 fresh basil leaves, chopped
55g (2oz) conchigliette (baby pasta shells) or wheat- or gluten-free pasta

1 Heat the oil in a saucepan and sauté the onion and carrot gently, stirring, for 3 minutes to soften. Add the garlic and sauté for a further 30 seconds.

2 Add the minced chicken and sauté, stirring, until it turns opaque and all the grains are separate.

3 Add the thyme, passata, and apple juice. Bring to the boil and stir in the tomato purée and Worcestershire sauce. Reduce the heat, cover, and simmer gently for 10 minutes. Stir in the basil.

4 Meanwhile, cook the pasta shells in boiling water according to the packet instructions. Drain and return to the pan. Stir in the sauce, cool slightly, and serve.

5 Freeze in individual portions. When needed, thaw overnight in the fridge or for 1-2 hours at room temperature, then microwave or reheat in a small pan until piping hot. Stir and allow to cool before serving.

Flex it...

Replace the chicken
with the equivalent amount of beef or lamb mince.

Chicken Bolognese

Made with baked sweet potato and cooked diced chicken, these delicious croquettes are the perfect size for little hands. They are deliciously soft and moist on the inside with a crispy golden coating. Serve with steamed veggies such as broccoli florets and mini carrots.

CHICKEN CROQUETTES

❄ **Suitable for freezing**

Makes 8 • Suitable from 9 months • Prep time 15 minutes • Cooking time 5 minutes
• Provides energy, protein, vitamin A • Dairy-free

1 small sweet potato
100g (3½oz) cooked chicken, diced
1 tsp chopped thyme leaves
2 spring onions, finely chopped
1–2 tsp soy sauce
1 tbsp sweet chilli sauce
40g (1½oz) panko breadcrumbs or gluten-free breadcrumbs – half in the mixture and half to coat
1 tbsp sunflower oil, for frying
Salt (for over 12 months) and freshly ground black pepper

1 Prick the sweet potato. Bake in the microwave for 10 minutes until soft. Alternatively, cook the sweet potato in a preheated oven to 180°C (fan 160°C), gas 4 for 30 minutes.

2 Leave the potato to cool, then scoop out the cold flesh – you will need about 100g (3½oz).

3 Place the potato in a bowl. Add the chicken, thyme, onions, sauces, 20g (¾oz) breadcrumbs, and the oil, and mix together. Lightly season, depending on your baby's age, and shape into eight little croquettes. Roll in the remaining 20g (¾oz) breadcrumbs.

4 Heat the oil in a frying pan. Add the croquettes and fry for about 5 minutes, until golden and crisp on all sides. Drain on kitchen paper and leave to cool before serving.

5 When needed, thaw overnight in the fridge or leave out for a few hours at room temperature. Reheat in an oven preheated to 180°C (fan 160°C), gas 4 for 10–12 minutes.

Red meat provides the best source of iron, the critical nutrient required for the production of haemoglobin, which carries oxygen to your baby's developing brain. It also supplies protein and zinc, essential for growth and a healthy immune system. You can freeze the sauce separately if you prefer and then serve it with rice or potato instead of pasta.

ANNABEL'S TASTY PASTA BOLOGNESE

❄ **Suitable for freezing**

Makes 4 portions • Suitable from 9 months • Prep time 10 minutes • Cooking time 30 minutes • Provides protein, iron, vitamin A, energy • Dairy-free

1 tbsp sunflower oil

1 small red onion, peeled and finely chopped

1 small carrot, peeled and grated

½ celery stick, strings removed and finely chopped

½ small eating apple, peeled and grated

4 tbsp water

200ml (7fl oz) passata (sieved tomatoes)

150g (5½oz) lean minced beef

1 small garlic clove, peeled and crushed

75ml (5 tbsp) unsalted beef or vegetable stock, or water

1 tsp chopped fresh thyme or ¼ tsp dried thyme

55g (2oz) conchigliette (baby pasta shells) or wheat- or gluten-free pasta

1 Heat the oil in a saucepan and gently sauté the onion, carrot, celery, and apple for 2 minutes. Add the water, stir, cover, and cook very gently for 8 minutes until soft.

2 Transfer the vegetables to a food processor, add the passata, and whizz until blended.

3 Meanwhile, dry-fry the minced beef in a non-stick frying pan. Add the garlic and sauté for 30 seconds.

4 Pour the tomato and vegetable sauce over the meat. Add the stock or water and the thyme, bring to the boil, reduce the heat, cover, and simmer gently for about 15 minutes until rich and tender.

5 Meanwhile, cook the pasta shells in boiling water according to the packet instructions. Drain and return to the pan. Stir in the sauce, cool slightly, and serve.

6 Freeze in individual portions. When required, thaw overnight in the fridge or for 1–2 hours at room temperature, then microwave or reheat in a small pan until piping hot. Stir and allow to cool before serving.

Self-feeding. Allow your baby to try to feed herself and try not to worry about the mess!

These tasty meatballs make perfect finger food on their own, but you can also serve them with the tomato and basil sauce used in the recipe on page 134.

MINI MEATBALLS

❄ **Suitable for freezing**

Makes 25 mini balls, 6–8 portions • Suitable from 9 months • Prep time 15 minutes • Cooking time 10 minutes • Provides energy, protein, iron, zinc, calcium

2 tsp olive oil

1 medium onion, peeled and finely chopped

1 garlic clove, peeled and crushed

200g (7oz) lean minced beef

45g (1½oz) fresh white breadcrumbs or wheat- or gluten-free alternative

1 tbsp chopped parsley

15g (½oz) Parmesan cheese, grated (see right)

1 tsp tomato purée

½ small eating apple, peeled and grated

¼ unsalted vegetable stock cube, crumbled

1 egg or egg replacement (see page 20)

Vegetable oil, for frying

1 Heat the oil in a saucepan and sauté the onion for 3 minutes, stirring, until softened. Add the garlic and sauté for 30 seconds. Set aside to cool.

2 Mix together the beef, breadcrumbs, parsley, Parmesan, tomato purée, apple, and stock cube. Stir in the sautéed onion and garlic, and add the beaten egg to bind.

3 Form the mixture into 25 mini meatballs. Heat the vegetable oil in a frying pan and sauté, until browned and cooked inside. Drain on kitchen paper.

4 To freeze, follow the instructions for freezing Annabel's Chicken Burgers on page 144.

For a dairy-free version, leave out the Parmesan cheese and add a beef stock cube.

Mini muffins are the perfect size for little hands. Banana and sultanas provide natural sweetness so you don't have to add much sugar.

REDUCED-SUGAR BANANA MUFFINS

⚙ **Suitable for freezing**

Makes 24 • Suitable from 9 months • Prep time 10 minutes • Cooking time 12 minutes
• Provides energy, protein, potassium, vitamin E, fibre • Dairy-free

1 banana, mashed
50g (1³/₄oz) light brown sugar
60ml (2fl oz) sunflower oil
1 egg, beaten, or egg
  replacement (see page 20)
150g (5¹/₂oz) self-raising flour
  or gluten-free flour
½ tsp baking powder
pinch of salt (only if
  over 12 months)
40g (1½oz) sultanas, chopped

1 Preheat the oven to 180°C (fan 160°C), gas 4. Line a 24-hole mini muffin tin with 24 mini muffin cases (or use two 12-hole muffin tins).

2 Mix the banana, sugar, oil, and egg together in a mixing bowl. Add the flour, baking powder, and salt, if using. Stir in the sultanas. Spoon into the cases.

3 Bake in the preheated oven for 12 minutes, until well risen and lightly golden brown. Cool on a wire rack.

4 Freeze in a plastic container with a lid and, when needed, defrost at room temperature for several hours.

Reduced-Sugar Banana Muffins

One of the most common food allergies among young children is to eggs (see page 20). These cookies are super-delicious even without the eggs, and they are perfect for self-feeding.

EGG-FREE SULTANA AND OAT COOKIES

❄ **Suitable for freezing**

Makes 15 • Suitable from 9 months • Prep time 10 minutes • Cooking time 12–15 minutes • Provides energy, fibre, iron

110g (3¾oz) soft unsalted butter or dairy-free spread
85g (3oz) light brown sugar
1 tsp vanilla extract
100g (3½oz) plain or gluten-free flour
100g (3½oz) porridge oats
½ tsp baking powder
pinch of salt (optional, if over 12 months)
50g (1¾oz) sultanas

1 Preheat the oven to 200°C (fan 180°C), gas 6. Line two baking sheets with non-stick paper.

2 Whisk the butter and sugar together in a bowl until light and fluffy.

3 Add the vanilla extract, flour, porridge oats, and baking powder, and a pinch of salt if using. Whisk the mixture until all the ingredients are fully combined.

4 Shape the mixture into 15 balls and place them, spaced out, on the baking tray. Flatten them down.

5 Bake in the preheated oven for 12–15 minutes until light brown in colour. Cool on a wire rack.

6 Freeze in a plastic container with a lid and, when needed, defrost at room temperature for several hours.

Flex it...

Replace the sultanas
with raisins, or do a mixture of half and half. Raisins are rich in fibre, vitamins, and minerals.

This quick and tasty layered dessert made with yogurt, cooked apples, and toasted oats will soon become a favourite – for your little one and probably for the whole family, too!

APPLE AND OAT SUNDAE

❄ **Not suitable for freezing**
Makes 4 portions • Suitable from 9 months • Prep time 10 minutes • Cooking time 10 minutes
• Provides energy, protein, fibre, calcium, vitamin C

20g (³/₄oz) butter or
  dairy-free spread
50g (1³/₄oz) jumbo oats
1 tsp brown sugar
¹/₄ tsp ground cinnamon
175g (6oz) Braeburn or
  Pink Lady apples, peeled,
  cored, and diced
2 tbsp orange juice
1 tsp maple syrup, plus
  4 tbsp for drizzling
250g (9oz) plain yogurt or
  dairy-free alternative

1 Melt half the butter in a frying pan. Add the oats and sugar and fry over a medium heat for a few minutes, stirring until the oats have turned golden brown. Leave to cool.

2 Sprinkle the ground cinnamon over the apple.

3 Heat the remaining butter in a saucepan. Add the apples, orange juice, and 1 teaspoon of maple syrup. Stir over a medium heat for 5 minutes until the apples have softened. Leave to cool.

4 Put 2 tablespoons of yogurt into the base of four small pots or glasses. Top with half of the apple mixture and drizzle with half of the maple syrup. Sprinkle half of the oats on top.

5 Repeat with another layer of yogurt, the remaining apple mixture, maple syrup, and oats so that you have two layers.

6 Chill in the fridge for 30 minutes before serving.

Flex it...

Use rhubarb in place of the apple. It is packed with vitamins and minerals, especially vitamin K.

Apple and Oat Sundae

Ice lollies are great for babies to suck on when they are teething. You could also make this lolly using orange juice instead of tropical fruit juice.

TROPICAL BANANA LOLLY

Makes 3–4 lollies • Suitable from 9 months • Prep time 5 minutes
• Provides calcium, potassium, vitamin C

½ small ripe banana
125g (4½oz) pot creamy
  vanilla full-fat yogurt or
  dairy-free alternative
100ml (3½fl oz) tropical
  fruit juice
1 tbsp icing sugar or agave
  or maple syrup (optional)

1 Blend the banana and yogurt until smooth in a food processor or place in a bowl and use a hand-blender. Add the fruit juice and sugar or syrup, if using, and blend until combined.

2 Pour into moulds and freeze for several hours or overnight.

Bursting with vitamins and minerals, these deliciously fresh lollies are a perfect way to make sure your baby gets the nutrients she needs.

BLUEBERRY AND BANANA LOLLY

Makes 4–5 lollies • Suitable from 9 months • Prep time 5 minutes
• Provides calcium, potassium, vitamin C

150g (5½oz) blueberries
6 tbsp creamy blueberry
  full-fat yogurt or
  dairy-free alternative
¼ ripe banana
1 tbsp icing sugar or agave
  or maple syrup (optional)

1 Blend the ingredients together until smooth in a food processor or use a hand-blender.

2 Pass through a sieve to remove the seeds and skins (if preferred, but not absolutely necessary). Pour into moulds and freeze overnight.

Tip:
If you don't have ice lolly containers, freeze the mixture in an ice-cube tray and stand a piece of plastic drinking straw up in the centre of each for the "stick". Each mixture will make between 12 and 18 cubes.

Flex it...

Blueberries can be swapped for any other berry in season, or why not try a blend?

Cool banana. Ice lollies provide a great way of getting some extra fruit into your baby at the same time as helping to soothe sore gums.

By now your baby will be eating the same foods as the rest of the family, albeit sometimes chopped. He'll also need a mid-morning and mid-afternoon snack (see page 125) and possibly an early-morning milk feed.

MENU PLANNER: 9 TO 12 MONTHS

DAY	BREAKFAST	LUNCH	MID AFTERNOON	TEA	BEDTIME
1	Egg, Spinach, and Tomato Muffin (p.132)/ fruit	Annabel's Tasty Pasta Bolognese (p.148)/yogurt	Breast/bottle and snack	Fish Fingers (p.140)/ baked sweet potato wedges/fruit	Breast/bottle
2	Wholegrain toast with peanut butter/ fruit	Annabel's Chicken Burger (p.144)/ sweet potato wedges/fruit	Breast/bottle and snack	Salmon, Squash, and Kale Balls (p.105)/ steamed vegetables/fruit	Breast/bottle
3	Purple Porridge (p.86) with dates/fruit	Mini Meatballs (p.150)/steamed broccoli and carrots/Fruit lolly (p.154)	Breast/bottle and snack	Chicken and Apple Balls (p.111)/fruit	Breast/bottle
4	Scrambled egg and toast fingers/fruit	Mini tuna or salmon sandwiches (see p.133)/dried apricots and fresh pear	Breast/bottle and snack	Cherub's Couscous (p.135); Apple and Oat Sundae (p.153)	Breast/bottle
5	Granola, fruit, and yogurt/ cheese	Annabel's Chicken Burger (p.144); burger bun, avocado, and red pepper/yogurt	Breast/bottle and snack	Mini Meatballs (p.150)/pasta/ carrots/ broccoli/fruit	Breast/bottle
6	Boiled egg with soldiers/ fruit	Chicken Croquettes (p.146)/ carrot sticks/ Sultana and Oat Cookies (p.152)	Breast/bottle and snack	Mini Fish Pie (p.138)/fruit	Breast/bottle
7	Iron-fortified breakfast cereal/yogurt/ fruit sticks	Sweet Potato and Kale Croquettes (p.90); Fruit lolly (p.154)	Breast/bottle and snack	Annabel's Tasty Pasta Bolognese (p.148); steamed vegetables/fruit	Breast/bottle

ABOUT THE AUTHOR

Annabel Karmel, MBE – Over 25 years of recipes and expert advice

London born mother of three Annabel Karmel has pioneered the way families all over the world feed their babies and children. Credited with starting a food revolution with her trusty recipes and methods, Annabel has become the UK's No.1 children's cookery author and bestselling international author with 45 cookbooks. In 2006, Annabel received an MBE in the Queen's Birthday Honours for her outstanding work in the field of child nutrition, and she is well recognized as one of the UK's leading female entrepreneurs.

With the sole mission of raising the standards of children's diets, Annabel is a sought-after media commentator on food-related issues, and she regularly undertakes consultancy work for major nursery chains, leisure resorts, restaurants, and hotels worldwide.

With millions of families relying on Annabel's recipes to raise healthy, happy babies, the feeding expert has cooked-up a brand new edition of her bestselling Baby & Toddler Recipe App. Packed with more than 220 delicious, nutritious recipes, simple planners, shopping lists, and more, it's the handiest of guides for easy mealtime inspiration – whether you're cooking for baby, toddler or the whole family. You'll also discover Annabel in the supermarket aisles with her nutritious Organic Baby Purées, Chilled Toddler Meals, and Frozen Kids Meals. Inspired by her most popular cookbook recipes, they taste just like you'd make at home – perfect for those busy days.

For lots more exclusive recipes, tips and advice, plus a host of great competitions and offers, join the AK Club for free today at www.annabelkarmel.com and be part of Annabel's world on social media too.

f annabelkarmeluk   **◉** annabelkarmel   **🐦** annabelkarmel

ACKNOWLEDGMENTS

First Edition

DK UK

Project editor Helen Murray
Editorial assistance Angela Baynham
Designer Jo Grey
Senior art editor Sara Kimmins
Jacket designer and design assistant Charlotte Seymour
Managing editor Penny Warren
Managing art editors Glenda Fisher and Marianne Markham
Senior production editor Jennifer Murray
Production controller Hema Gohil
Creative technical support Sonia Charbonnier
Category publisher Peggy Vance
Editorial consultant Karen Sullivan
Allergy consultant Dr Adam Fox
Nutritional consultant Dr Rosan Meyer
Food styling Seiko Hatfield
Home economist Carolyn Humphries
Photographer Dave King
Photography art direction Peggy Sadler

Second Edition

Author's Acknowledgments
Special thanks to Sarah Almond Bushell MPhil BSc (Hons) Registered Dietitian for her expert nutritional advice. A big thank you to the wonderful team involved in producing this book: Mary-Clare Jerram, Lucinda McCord, Ian Hudson, Dawn Bates, Dawn Henderson, Marianne Markham, Saffron Stocker, Philippa Nash, Jonathan Lloyd, Dave King, and Peggy Vance. With thanks to Tripp Trapp for supplying a high chair.

Publisher's Acknowledgments
DK would like to thank Bharti Karakoti and Vinita Venugopal for design assistance, Megan Lea for editorial assistance, Claire Cross for proofreading, and Shirley May for the index.

Picture Credits
The publisher would like to thank the following for their kind permission to reproduce their photographs:

(Key: a-above; b-below/bottom; c-centre; f-far; l-left; r-right; t-top)

38, 39, 40 Annabel Karmel; 39 Stokke; Tripp Trapp® by Stokke® www.stokke.com (cra)

All other images © Dorling Kindersley
For further information see: www.dkimages.com

INDEX

INDEX

WEANING RESOURCES

BabyCentre
www.babycentre.co.uk

National Childcare Trust
www.nct.org.uk

Tesco Baby Club
www.tesco-baby.com

Allergy

Allergy UK
www.allergyuk.org

Anaphylaxis Campaign
www.anaphylaxis.org.uk.

Breastfeeding

Association of Breastfeeding Mothers
www.abm.me.uk

Breastfeeding Network
www.breastfeedingnetwork.org.uk

La Leche League
www.laleche.org.uk

Equipment

Mothercare
www.mothercare.com

Nutrition and health

British Dietetic Association
www.bda.uk.com

British Nutrition Foundation
www.nutrition.org.uk

Food Standards Agency
www.food.gov.uk

Vegan Society
www.vegansociety.com.

Vegetarian Society
www.vegsoc.org

Penguin
Random
House

DK LONDON
Senior Editor Dawn Bates
Senior Designer Saffron Stocker
Designer Philippa Nash
Jacket Designer Steven Marsden
Pre-Production Producer Rob Dunn
Producer Ché Creasey
Managing Editor Dawn Henderson
Managing Art Editor Marianne Markham
Art Director Maxine Pedliham
Publishing Director Mary-Clare Jerram
Food Stylist Tamara Vos
Prop Stylist Rob Merrett
Photographer Dave King

DK INDIA
Senior Editor Arani Sinha
Assistant Editors Rishi Bryan,
Devangana Ojha, Nonita Saha
Senior Art Editor Chhaya Sajwan
Art Editors Sourabh Challariya, Shipra Jain
Assistant Art Editor Amrai Dua
Managing Editor Soma B. Chowdhury
Senior Managing Art Editor Arunesh Talapatra
Senior DTP Designer Tarun Sharma
DTP Designer Satish Gaur
Pre-production Manager Sunil Sharma

Every effort has been made to ensure that the information contained in this book is complete and accurate. However, neither the publisher nor the author are engaged in rendering professional advice or services to the individual reader. The ideas, procedures, and suggestions contained in the book are not intended as a substitute for consultation with your healthcare provider. All matters regarding the health of you and your child require medical supervision. Neither the publisher nor the author accept any legal responsibility for any personal injury or other damage or loss arising from the use or misuse of the information and advice in this book.

This edition published in 2018
First published in Great Britain in 2010 by
Dorling Kindersley Limited
80 Strand, London, WC2R 0RL

Copyright © 2010, 2018 Dorling Kindersley Limited, London
A Penguin Random House Company
Text copyright © 2010, 2018 Annabel Karmel

10 9 8 7 6 5 4 3 2 1
001–311196–Aug/2018

A CIP catalogue of this book
is available from the British Library.

ISBN 978-0-2413-5248-9

Printed and bound in China
A WORLD OF IDEAS:
SEE ALL THERE IS TO KNOW

www.dk.com

Weaning Resources